TO WIN THE

HOME FRONT MEMORABILIA
OF WORLD WAR II

Johnny Noble was one of
the most popular band
leaders and songwriters
in Hawaii in the 1920s
and 30s. He conducted
the Moana Hotel
Orchestra for many years

TO WIN THE WAR

HOME FRONT MEMORABILIA
OF WORLD WAR II

FROM THE COLLECTIONS OF:

Gary Skoloff, Martin Jacobs, Jack Matthews,
Jim Osborne, Ken Fleck, Merv Bloch and Stan Cohen

Pictorial Histories Publishing Co. Inc.
Missoula, Montana

COPYRIGHT ©1995 PICTORIAL HISTORIES PUBLISHING CO. INC.

LIBRARY OF CONGRESS
CATALOG CARD NUMBER 95-69532

ISBN 1-57510-000-2

First Printing: July 1995

Prepress Layout by:
Prepress Plus, Missoula, Montana
Cover Graphics by:
Mike Egeler
Printed by Publishers Press
Shepherdsville, Kentucky

Printed in U.S.A.

Book Trade Distribution by:

Motorbooks International
Publishers & Wholesalers ®

PICTORIAL HISTORIES PUBLISHING CO. INC.
713 So. Third Street
Missoula, Montana 59801

Introduction

I consider this book a companion volume to my 1991 edition, *V For Victory, America's Home Front During World War II*. This is certainly not a definitive book on memorabilia considering the millions of items produced from 1939 to 1945. Nor is it a price guide as it would be difficult to set prices on many of the one-of-a-kind items included. I would treat this book as a nostalgic trip back into the time of five decades ago and also as a teaching aid for people who did not live during those times.

It is fitting that this book be produced just before the 50th anniversary of the end of what Studs Turkel called "The Good War." My *V For Victory* came out just before the 50th anniversary of the beginning of America's involvement in the war in December 1991.

Many books, including some I have written or published (see the selected bibliography) have covered portions of this book in some detail. However, I believe this is the greatest accumulation of home front memorabilia compiled into one volume.

The collections from which this material has been drawn are large and in most cases museum quality. Gary Skoloff's collection, while stored in his attic, is immense with a heavy emphasis on paper items. Marty Jacobs may have the largest V for Victory collection in the country. Ken and Mady Fleck's anti-Axis collection is large and unusual in nature. Jack Matthews' collection of World War II toys is just one part of his massive toy collection. (I recently published a book just on his wartime toys.) Jim Osborne has collected so many military items that he founded the Indiana Military Museum in his hometown of Vincennes, Indiana, to house them. Merv Block has a pristine collection of wartime bubble gum cards and German military tin toys. My collection, while quite small, has served as a sort of seed for getting these large collections together.

I think if this book teaches us anything it is the level of home front propaganda used against the Axis powers, and in particular, Hitler, Tojo and Mussolini, and even against Stalin before Germany's invasion of Russia in June 1941. How times and allegiances have changed in the past 50 years.

This book would not be possible without the photographic expertise of Allan Reider of Union, New Jersey, who photographed over 300 items from Skoloff's collection and Garry L. Hall of Vincennes, Indiana, who photographed Osborne's collection. Lanny and Ann Bryant and Lady Russ of Prepress +Plus of Missoula took my layout ideas and did a fantastic job getting the book ready for the printer. I want to again thank all the contributors to this book and hope it helps the general public to understand the great feeling of patriotic pride that all Americans felt for their country in the trying days of World War II.

If only we all had this same feeling today.

Stan Cohen
Publisher
July 1995

"The country that ceases to embrace its heritage and tradition, loses its identity"
Winston Churchill

Contents

Not at War, Not at Peace

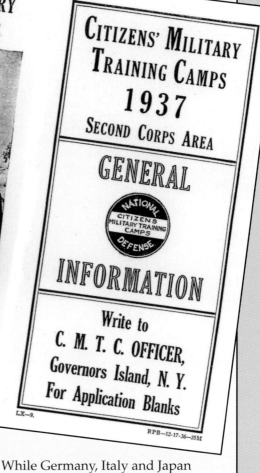

CITIZENS' MILITARY TRAINING CAMPS FOR 1937

For New York, New Jersey, Delaware

Mission of the C. M. T. C.

Citizens' Military Training Camps are authorized by Congress to be held under the auspices of the War Department at various places throughout the United States each summer. They are a part of the general scheme of National Defense, but the military side of the camps is by no means the only one, nor is the development of soldiers the real objective of Congress or the War Department. They are placed under the War Department because it is the only department with the necessary personnel and because military training is the best means of accomplishing the objects of the camps. The purpose is to develop the manhood of the Nation by bringing together young men of high and different types, both native and foreign born, from all sections of the country, on a common basis of equality and under the most favorable conditions of outdoor life; to teach them the privileges, duties and responsibilities of American citizenship; to stimulate the interest of the youth of this country in the importance of military training as a benefit to the Nation and the individual taking such training; to inculcate self-discipline and obedience; and to develop these young men physically, mentally and morally.

Origin of the Camps

The Citizens' Military Training Camps are the direct outgrowth of the original Plattsburg Camps of 1913, 1914 and 1915, which were initiated by General Leonard Wood and heartily endorsed by Ex-President Roosevelt, and have been supported by leading citizens everywhere. The experiences of the Draft during the World War revealed an unexpectedly large proportion of rejections for physical reasons. Army medical officers and civilian physicians maintain that a great proportion of these physical defects could have been corrected and cured if recognized and treated in time. Bearing these facts in mind, Congress, in the National Defense Act of 1920, authorized the

camps, and the first Citizens' Military Training Camp was held in 1921 with an attendance of 10,299. Since then, more than half a million young men have attended these camps. A remarkable change has come in our national life through emphasis on proper diet, exercise and outdoor living. The characteristic American gospel of health and fitness brings to the camps thousands who are not eager to shine as athletes, but seek the conditions which make for bodily well being. Young men have caught the spirit and have adopted what may be called almost a religion of physical health. The C. M. T. Camps are, in the words of Ex-President Coolidge, "essentially schools in citizenship." They are, it is true, an indispensable factor in the maintenance of the National Defense Act. They are contributing an important percentage of the membership of the Officers' Reserve Corps. But above all, the men, who have attended the camps, have carried to every community of the United States, a new reverence for the flag, coupled with high determination to do their duty as citizens. Patriotism and devotion to country are the first fruits of the Citizens' Camps and these qualities are backed by physical vigor, mental alertness and higher sense of responsibility.

Courses of Training
(See Application Blank)

The camps are conducted in a series of four courses, known as the Basic, Red, White and Blue, and must be taken in that order by the candidates. The camps are held in the summer and are of thirty days duration. The military training is progressive through the four years. After satisfactorily completing the Basic Course, and before entering the Red Course, the candidate selects the branch of the service in which he wants to be trained for the next three years from the following: Infantry, Field Artillery or Coast Artillery. Graduation from the Blue Course does not of itself, however, confer legal eligibility for a Reserve Commission. In addition, for appointment in the Officers' Reserve Corps, there are also necessary enlistment in the Enlisted Reserve Corps or Regular Army and satisfactory completion of examination, by a board of officers in those prescribed subjects not covered in the Blue Course. There is no obligation, expressed or implied, to accept a commission, or even go to camp the second, third or fourth summer, unless the candidate so desires.

In the Basic and Red Courses mornings are devoted to military drill and instruction, and afternoons, except

While Germany, Italy and Japan were rearming in the 1930s the United States had only a very limited rearmament program and a small professional military. The military buildup in the United States increased rapidly in 1940 and 1941, despite the country's professed neutrality. The National Guard was called up in 1940 for federal duty, and the first peacetime draft took place in October 1940. The Pacific fleet was moved from its home port in California to Hawaii in order to "show the flag" closer to the western Pacific and hopefully thwart Japanese aggression. Defense industries geared up not only to supply increased American military demands but also to supply the besieged nations of Europe.

This magazine issue is from January 1939, eight months before Germany attacked Poland, but war clouds covered most of Europe for the last years of the 1930s.

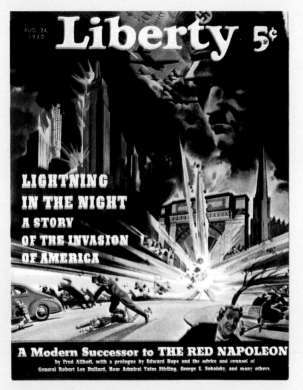

This issue is from August 1940 when most of Europe had been overrun by German forces. America was still neutral but getting more involved day by day.

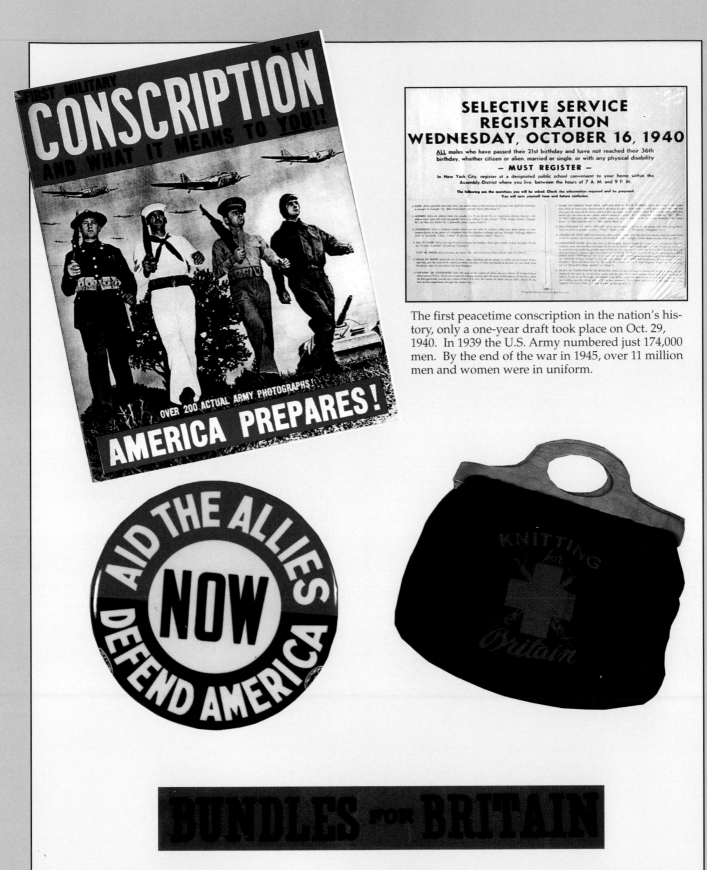

The first peacetime conscription in the nation's history, only a one-year draft took place on Oct. 29, 1940. In 1939 the U.S. Army numbered just 174,000 men. By the end of the war in 1945, over 11 million men and women were in uniform.

Bundles For Britain was founded by Mrs. Walls Latham on Jan. 15, 1940. Its purpose was to provide non-military aid to the British people who were beseiged by the German military forces. Items such as medicine, clothing and blankets were collected from American citizens and shipped to Britain.

The America First Committee was organized by isolationists on Sept. 4, 1940, to counter the growing involvement of the United States in the European conflict. One strong catalyst for the committee to organize was the destroyer for bases trade two days before between Britain and the United States.

As the months of 1940 and 1941 passed by it became harder and harder for the committee to convince the nation to adhere to a neutrality policy as the Axis powers proceeded to overrun country after country. The Pearl Harbor attack, of course, put an end to the committee's activities.

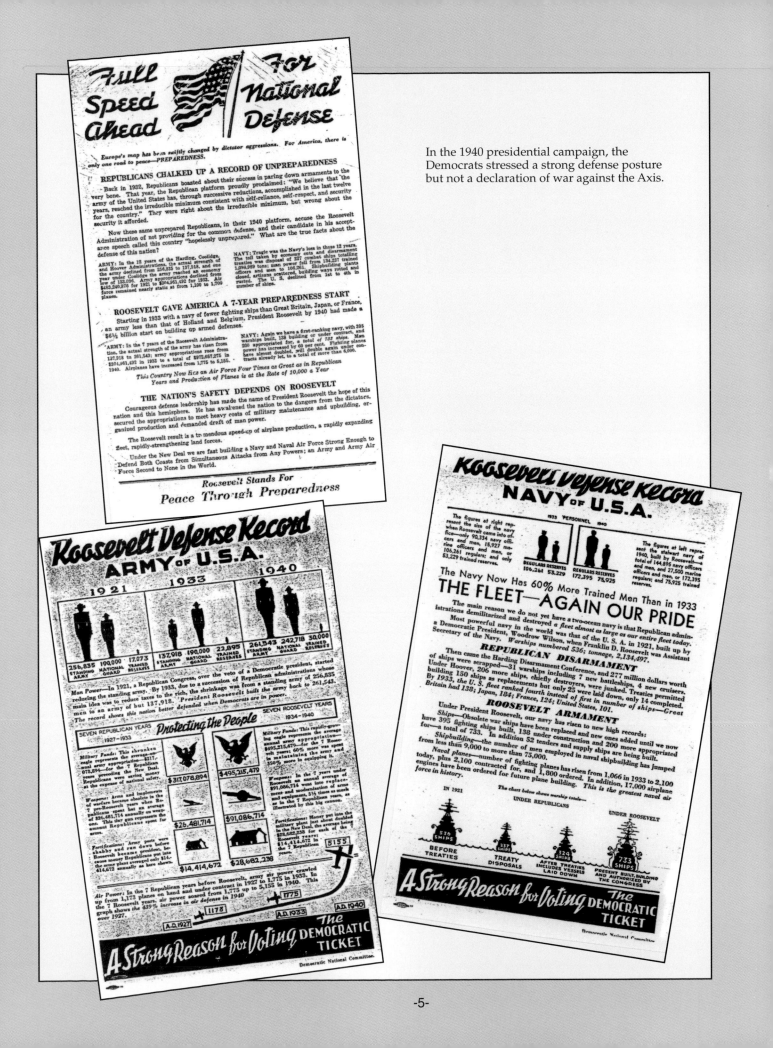

In the 1940 presidential campaign, the Democrats stressed a strong defense posture but not a declaration of war against the Axis.

Envelopes from 1941.

The German army invaded Russia in June 1941 with spectacular results but got bogged down in the winter of 1941 without capturing Moscow or the Russian oil fields.

The United State supplied Britain with military aid through the Lend-Lease Program before her own entry into the war in December 1941.

The German Air Force bombed England mercilessly but could not win the Battle of Britain.

The Italian army invaded Greece in 1941 but had to be rescued by Hitler. The Italians also were driven out of East Africa by the British and had to be rescued again by the Germans in North Africa.

Remember Pearl Harbor

America has had significant events or incidents that have carried into wars since the 1840s. *Remember the Alamo* was the rallying cry for soldiers in the Mexican War of 1846, commemorating the famous Alamo battle in 1836 for Texas Independence. *Remember the Maine* was on the lips of troops disembarking on Cuban soil in the summer of 1898 to throw out the Spaniards from the island. The *USS Maine*, anchored in Havana's harbor was blown up in February 1898 supposedly by Spanish saboteurs. (It is now thought that the ship was probably destroyed by spontaneous combustion in its fuel supply). The British ship *Lusitania* was sunk by a German U-Boat in 1915 killing a number of American citizens. Although America did not enter the First World War until two years later, the *Lusitania* was never forgotten by citizens clamoring for war with Germany.

America managed to stay out of the Second World War for almost three years although her navy was battling the German submarine menace in the Atlantic, and sustaining casualties and committing her massive production to Allied Lend-Lease before the Dec. 7, 1941 attack on Pearl Harbor.

The sneak attack on Hawaii on that fateful Sunday morning was perhaps the greatest rallying point around which America would gather in its 165 year history. The *Remember Pearl Harbor* theme was carried out throughout the war in every facet of propaganda until the Japanese finally surrendered in August 1945.

The theme is still with us today whenever someone protests the downsizing of the military or feels inclined to do some Japanese bashing. It's a controversy that lives with us today - who knew or didn't know what - with countless theories written about the attack.

The following artifacts are representations of the lengths to which this theme was carried out by and for the American people decrying the war.

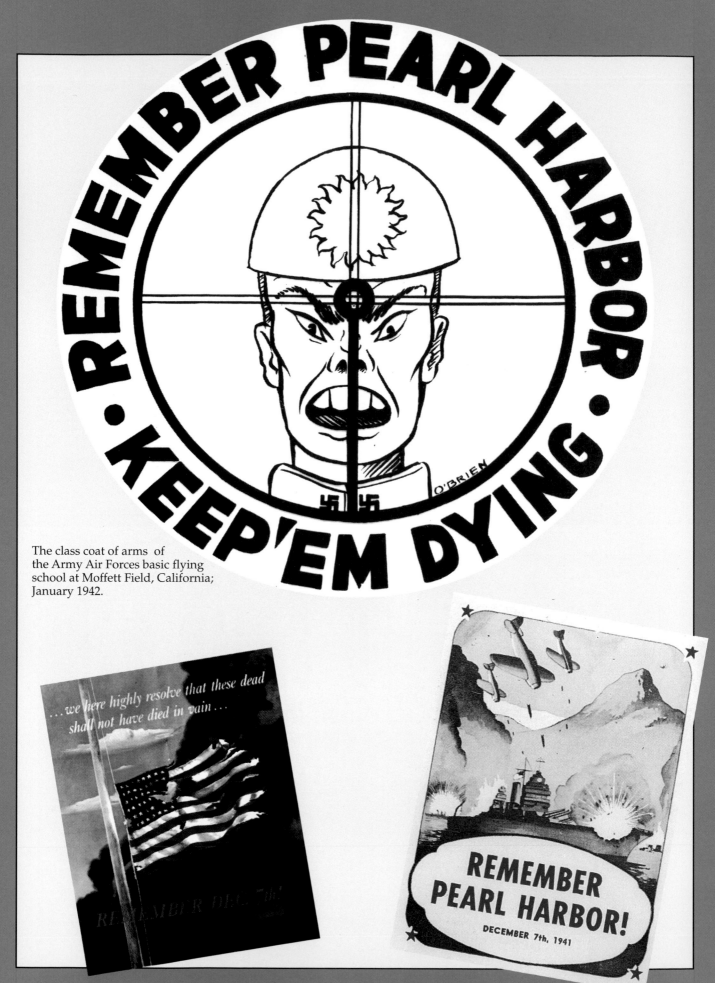

The class coat of arms of the Army Air Forces basic flying school at Moffett Field, California; January 1942.

This envelope is interesting as it's dated Dec. 11, 1941, four days after Pearl Harbor. It was addressed to China, at that time occupied by the Japanese. After December 7, of course, there was no mail delivery across the Pacific.

This vicious anti-Japanese booklet was published in early 1941 by Street & Smith Publications, Inc. It is interesting reading for the intense propaganda message and the inaccuracies that were not known at the time.

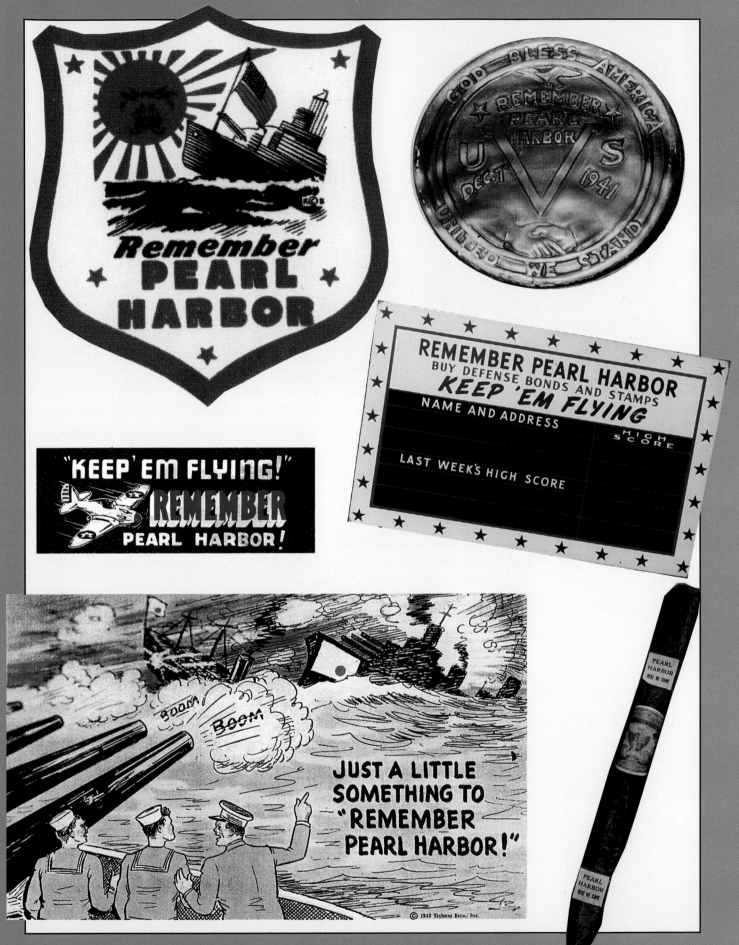

Pins and Covers

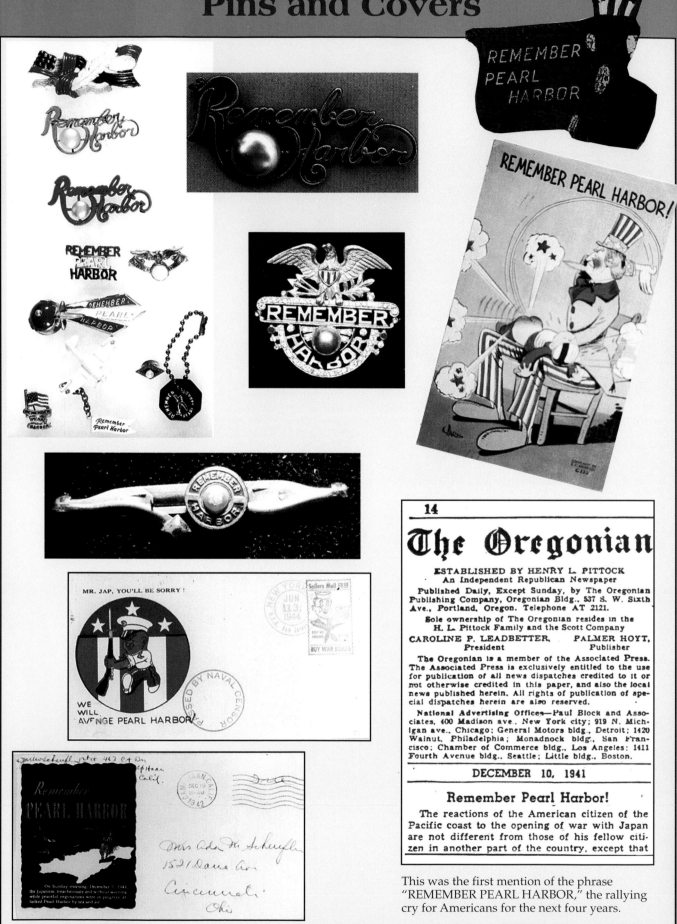

The Oregonian

ESTABLISHED BY HENRY L. PITTOCK
An Independent Republican Newspaper
Published Daily, Except Sunday, by The Oregonian Publishing Company, Oregonian Bldg., 537 S. W. Sixth Ave., Portland, Oregon. Telephone AT 2121.

Sole ownership of The Oregonian resides in the H. L. Pittock Family and the Scott Company

CAROLINE P. LEADBETTER,   PALMER HOYT,
President   Publisher

The Oregonian is a member of the Associated Press. The Associated Press is exclusively entitled to the use for publication of all news dispatches credited to it or not otherwise credited in this paper, and also the local news published herein. All rights of publication of special dispatches herein are also reserved.

National Advertising Offices—Paul Block and Associates, 400 Madison ave., New York city; 919 N. Michigan ave., Chicago; General Motors bldg., Detroit; 1420 Walnut, Philadelphia; Monadnock bldg., San Francisco; Chamber of Commerce bldg., Los Angeles; 1411 Fourth Avenue bldg., Seattle; Little bldg., Boston.

DECEMBER 10, 1941

Remember Pearl Harbor!

The reactions of the American citizen of the Pacific coast to the opening of war with Japan are not different from those of his fellow citizen in another part of the country, except that

This was the first mention of the phrase "REMEMBER PEARL HARBOR," the rallying cry for Americans for the next four years.

Early Battles and Heroes

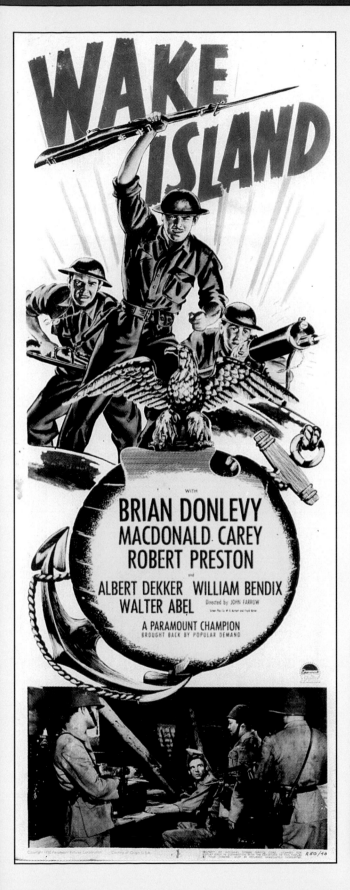

WAKE ISLAND

Wake Island is a three-square mile island several thousand miles west of Hawaii. Over 400 US Marines and over 1,000 civilian contractors were building up the island's defenses when the Japanese attacked on Dec. 8, 1941. In a heroic 16-day battle, the island's defenders put up a gallant struggle until forced to surrender on Dec. 24. The survivors, except for 98 civilians were taken to Japan for internment. The 98 civilians, were executed in 1943. *Remember Wake Island* became a rallying cry for all Americans and especially the US Marines through the rest of the war.

The Movie "Wake Island"

Just four months after the island's fall, filming began on the movie "Wake Island." Although its production was delayed a few weeks on the slim hope that the island would be recaptured, the movie was the first Hollywood film after the Pearl Harbor attack that attempted to portray accurately American fighting men.

The Paramount Pictures film was directed by ex-Marine John Farrow with a screenplay by W.R. Burnett and Frank Butler. It featured some notable film actors of the day: MacDonald Carey, Robert Preston, William Bendix, Walter Abel, Rod Cameron and Barbara Britton.

The film, which was first shown before 2,000 Marines at Quantico in August 1942, was very popular and had a great impact on the promotion of the war effort. It also received three Oscar nominations.

BRIAN DONLEVY
MACDONALD CAREY
ROBERT PRESTON

WAKE ISLAND

ALBERT DEKKER
WILLIAM BENDIX
WALTER ABEL
DIRECTED BY JOHN FARROW
Screen Play by W. R. Burnett and Frank Butler
A PARAMOUNT PICTURE

America's First War Souvenir

This two-man midget submarine was the only one of five that was captured after the Pearl Harbor attack. It was beached near Bellows Field on Oahu's east side. One of its two crewman, Ensign Kazuo Sakamaki survived and was the first Japanese prisoner of World War II. The sub was brought to the United States and sent around the country to help sell war bonds. It is now on display at the Admiral Nimitz Museum State Historical Park in Fredericksburg, Texas.

Coming Soon!

CAPTURED 2-MAN JAP SUB

SEE YOUR NEWS-PAPERS ★ LISTEN TO YOUR RADIO FOR LOCAL DETAILS ★

JAP SUICIDE SUBMARINE

MILITARY PARK
TUESDAY, APRIL 27, 1943

MILLION DOLLAR WAR BOND HOUR

SPECIAL PREVIEW 10 A.M. - 11 A.M.

SPONSORED BY

★ THE NEWARK WAR BOND COMMITTEE ★

Doolittle's Tokyo Raid April 18, 1942

One of the most daring actions of the war took place on Apr. 18, 1942 when 16 B-25 bombers took off from the *USS Hornet*, 624 miles from Japan and bombed Tokyo and other cities. It was a surprise attack, conducted to avenge Pearl Harbor and lift the spirits of the American people. Fifteen planes made it to China but all crashed, one landed safely in Russia. Lt. Colonel Jimmy Doolittle led the raid and was promoted to Brigadier General and awarded the Medal of Honor.

Cards were inserted in Kellogg's cereal boxes for kids to collect along with the appropriate stamps.

First Bombing of Tokyo The Japanese couldn't believe it—till the bombs fell—but the Americans *had* bombed Tokyo! With superb skill, Jimmy Doolittle did what had never been done before—flew long-range bombers from the deck of a carrier at sea. Into the heart of Japan they flew, bearing the first of the thousands of tons of bombs to hit Japan. With superb Navy seamanship, and great Army flying, the job that "couldn't be done" *was* done on April 18, 1942, scarcely more than 4 months after Pearl Harbor.

Coral Sea The Japanese were ready to advance into Southeast New Guinea, and began to concentrate ships for the push. In May, 1942, the first American task force contact was made, surprising and all but destroying 12 warships and transports at Tulagi. Three days later, planes from 3 U.S. carriers found a large Japanese force in the Coral Sea, and sank one carrier, and four cruisers, plus other ships. The old carrier Lexington was wounded and was lost because of internal explosions.

First in battle at the Coral Sea, and then at Midway, the Grumman TBF Avenger is a versatile torpedo bomber that can operate either from a carrier or land base.

The Jap way—
COLD-BLOODED MURDER

Japs Execute Group of Tokyo Air Raiders

We'll make them pay if you keep up
PRODUCTION

Eight raiders were captured after they crashed in China. Three were executed, one died in captivity and four survived the war. This poster shows captive Lt. Bobby Hite being led away by the Japanese. He was one of the survivors.

Newspapers around the world headlined the historic raid on Japan.

Doolittle was the subject of several bubble gum cards. He became commander of air forces in North Africa, Europe and Okinawa.

GEN. JAMES H. DOOLITTLE

Doolittle Receives Congressional Medal
© Gum, Inc.

Do More for Doolittle

The Movie "Thirty Seconds Over Tokyo"

Ted Lawson, pilot of plane #7 lost his leg as a result of the raid. He wrote the book, *Thirty Seconds Over Tokyo*, which was made into a 1944 movie starring Spencer Tracy, Van Johnson, Robert Mitchum, Robert Walker and Phyllis Thaxter. It was produced by Sam Zimbalist and directed by Mervyn LeRoy.

The Legend of Colin Kelly

Colin Kelly was America's first hero of the war but not the way he was portrayed during and for many years after the war. Kelly was the pilot of a B-17 bomber that supposedly dropped three bombs on the Japanese battleship, *Haruna*, on Dec. 10, 1941. His bomber was then shot up by Japanese fighters and he ordered his crew to bail out and then crash landed. He did not survive. For this action he was posthumously awarded the Distinguished Service Cross. Kelly was even reported to have flown his plane "down the funnels of the *Haruna*," which was totally false. Kelly's plane did bomb a Japanese cruiser, the *Ashigara*, but did not sink her. Captain Kelly, under heavy fire and with his aircraft in flame, ordered his crew to bail out. Kelly remained with the aircraft and it exploded in mid-air. America needed a quick hero after the disastrous Pearl Harbor and Philippines attacks and Kelly was a perfect candidate--West Point graduate, pilot who saved his crew and supposedly heroically crash landed into an enemy battleship.

V For Victory

A World War II Icon

In a radio broadcast from London on January 14, 1941, a Belgian refugee urged people of all oppressed nations during World War II to undermine Axis morale by waving two fingers in a V shape. Soon after, the V sign incorporated the Morse code--*dot, dot, dot, dash*--with the sound.

The British and Americans were helped a great deal by the French underground. The Resistance, as the Underground was known, was ordered to disrupt the German military through coded messages broadcast from England. Rather than send a message back to England and be detected, the French adapted a system through a regular broadcast station to let the Allies know that the orders were executed according to plan--mission completed.

This was done by playing Beethoven's Fifth Symphony soon after the assignment was finished. Why Beethoven's Fifth? Well, it starts out "dit, dit, dit, dah"--Morse code for "V," which also means "victory." This musical message was never decoded by the Germans.

After the surprise attack on Pearl Harbor, Americans in the United States staged wild recruiting rallies, cheering our departing GIs, singing patriotic songs and dancing the Victory Polka. With patriotism at a fever pitch, the "V for Victory" sign could be seen everywhere. It soon became an icon in support of our troops.

Though battles were taking place far from U.S. borders--on Pacific islands, in Europe and in North Africa--the war was never far from anyone's mind.

In the midst of the war, over one million babies were born. It was a common sight to see the V sign on baby carriages and even diapers. It was fashionable to be patriotic and Americans of all ages were put on notice that the "V for Victory" propaganda was good for everyone.

At the request of the U.S. Treasury Department, animator Walt Disney designed V emblems, casting Disney stars Donald Duck and Mickey Mouse to promote collecting of U.S. Saving Stamps.

During the war, farmers were busy growing food for our troops. But on the home front, food was in short supply. The Secretary of Agriculture told Americans that if they wanted fresh vegetables on their tables, they should plant "victory gardens" using "victory seeds."

Victory gardens sprang up in unlikely places like Chicago's Arlington Racetrack, the Portland (OR.) Zoo, and even on the prison island of Alcatraz near San Francisco. In Tennessee, farmers who grew 75 percent or more of their own food received a "V Certificate" ("Vitamins for Victory") from the government.

In the windows of nearly every patriotic American home hung a banner reading "This is a Victory Home." Inside, a "V Home Certificate" was usually displayed in a prominent place. To qualify for this government certificate, the family had to comply with the instructions of the air-raid warden regarding protection and blackouts, and purchase U.S. War Savings Bonds.

The Automobile Club of America distributed V auto tags that clipped onto a license plate and a sticker that read "Drive for Victory." Drivers were encouraged to follow a vehicle program toward preserving the transportation system of America.

Even comic strip characters got involved. Comic character Joe Palooka joined the Army and wore the Victory Task force patch on his uniform. Little Orphan Annie persuaded real kids to hand out leaflets proliferating the "V."

During the war, the government encouraged letter writing to our troops as it boosted their morale. Because of the enormous number of letters and postcards mailed, the U.S. Army Postal Service introduced "V-Mail." By microfilming letters onto negatives, or film reels, precious cargo space was saved. Once the reels arrived, they were printed by postal officials and delivered at home or abroad.

Major airlines turned over 50 percent of their planes to the Army Transport Command to deliver food and supplies to our troops. Painted on the fuselage of DC-3 cargo planes was "Victory Velocity." On American Airlines' domestic flights, the V design was printed on their place settings, napkins, glasses and cups.

At a Bomber Command Base, usually called "Boom Town," bombardiers carefully painted the V sign on the nose fuse pocket of the bombs, then gave the "thumbs up" for "bombs away."

The most popular V item during the war was the V dress pin and pinback button. It was made for men, women and children and worn around the clock at home, by employees in department stores, and at work in the defense plants. Slogans like "Buy Victory Bonds, V-Food for Freedom, V for Victory" and "V Stars and Stripes Forever" were most commonly seen.

The dress pins were made of plastic, pewter, copper, brass, sterling silver, pot metal, marcasite and gold. They were encrusted with pearls, rhinestones, amethysts and diamonds which were adorned with eagles, lions and flags flanking the V.

Today, a "V for Victory" memento is a valued treasure. Occasionally, an item can be found at a collector's show, antique shop, military shop, in an auction catalog, or at a flea market or garage sale--or even in a dresser drawer in the attic.

-Martin Jacobs-

Victory Pins

VICTORY PINS were usually worn by women in the defense plants. They were adorned on their overalls, dresses, suits, coats, and even their hats. The plastic V pin was typically worn by clerks in department stores. The pins were made either from sterling silver, gold, pewter, copper, celluloid or marcasite. There were enameled pins studded with rhinestones or jeweled with amethyst, topaz or diamonds. And most V pins were marked with three dots and a dash, symbolizing the Morse code for Victory. The V pins sparked patriotism everywhere they were worn.

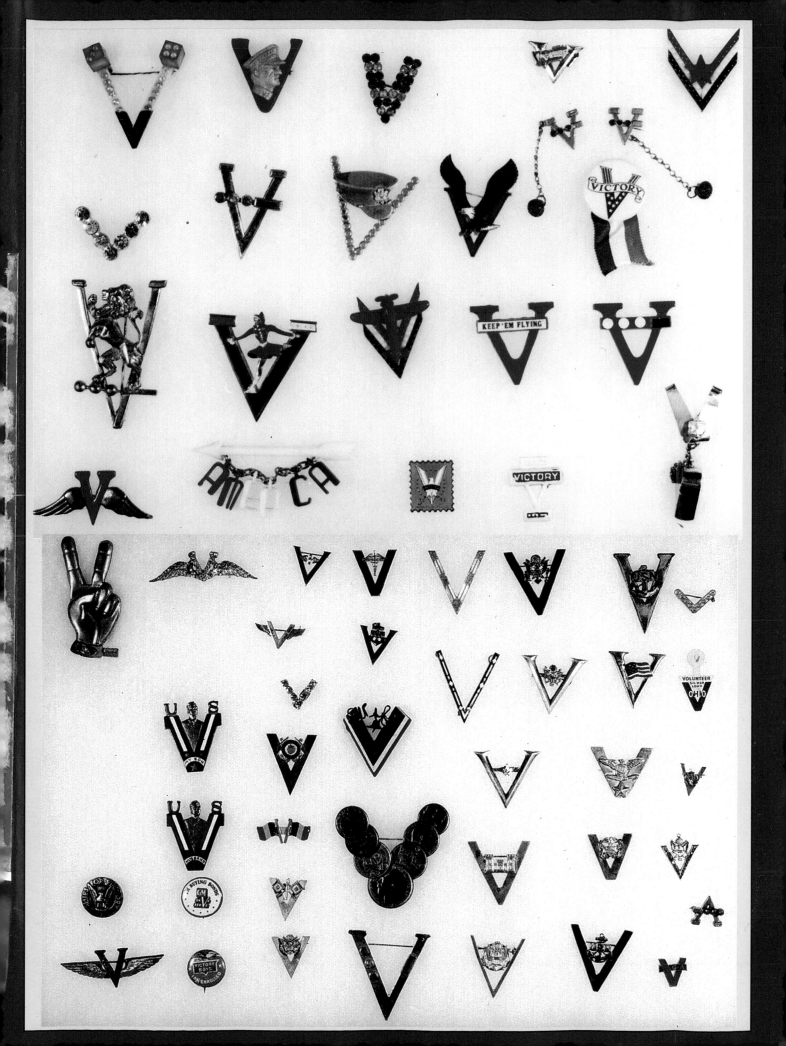

This is an unusual pin as it depicts Olympic skating star and movie actress, Sonja Henie, who met Hitler at the 1936 Winter Olympics in Germany.

One of a series of patriotic V glasses.

A rare chicken box, still in pristine condition.

Salt and pepper shakers.

A cardboard lunch box.

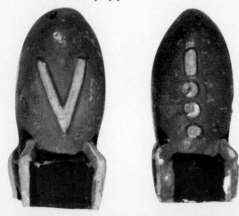

PROPAGANDA

Bubble Gum Cards

Bubble gum cards appealed to kids before and during the war, just as they do today. Gum Inc. of Philadelphia and its "Blony" gum instituted a series of 240 cards in 1938 depicting the Japanese atrocities in their war with China. Gum's advertising counsel, a Sunday school teacher named George Maull, put a peaceful tone to each card-- "To know the Horrors of War is to want Peace."

The cards are very graphic and on the back of each is a detailed caption of the Japanese atrocities. Japan had been battling the Chinese since the early 1930s and formerly declared war in 1937. By 1941 most of the Chinese coast had been occupied by Japanese forces.

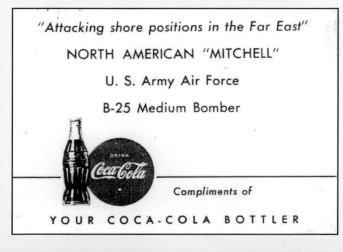

"Attacking shore positions in the Far East"

NORTH AMERICAN "MITCHELL"

U. S. Army Air Force

B-25 Medium Bomber

DRINK Coca-Cola

Compliments of

YOUR COCA-COLA BOTTLER

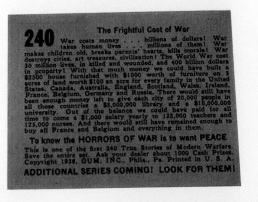

240 The Frightful Cost of War

War costs money . . . billions of dollars! War takes human lives . . . millions of them! War makes children old, breaks parents' hearts, kills morale! War destroys cities, art treasures, civilization! The World War cost 30 million lives, in killed and wounded, and 400 billion dollars in property! With that much money we could have built a $2500 house furnished with $1000 worth of furniture on 5 acres of land worth $100 an acre for every family in the United States, Canada, Australia, England, Scotland, Wales, Ireland, France, Belgium, Germany and Russia. There would still have been enough money left to give each city of 20,000 people in all those countries a $5,000,000 library and a $10,000,000 university. Out of the balance we could have paid for all time to come a $1,000 salary yearly to 125,000 teachers and 125,000 nurses. And there would still have remained enough to buy all France and Belgium and everything in them.

To know the HORRORS OF WAR is to want PEACE

This is one of the first 240 True Stories of Modern Warfare. Save the entire set. Ask your dealer about 1000 Cash Prizes. Copyright 1938, GUM, INC., Phila., Pa. Printed in U. S. A.

ADDITIONAL SERIES COMING! LOOK FOR THEM!

60   Flame-Throwers

Although no mention has been made of liquid fire in the early stages of the present conflict, it is a war device, developed by the Germans during the World War, that may be used. The picture shows an imaginary battalion of flame-throwers, dressed in asbestos suits, going to work on the enemy. The liquid fire is a highly inflammable oil ignited from a blow pipe. The portable flame-thrower shown has a range of 45 yards.

WAR NEWS PICTURES

Keep a permanent record of the current war in Europe. Don't miss any of these important historical pictures. Copyright 1939, GUM, INC., Phila., Pa. Printed in U.S.A.

C-19-72

59   "Air Infantry"

The transporting of troops by plane, developed by Russia in 1936, has more recently been taken up by other countries now at war including the major powers. In the picture, infantrymen armed with rifles and sub-machine guns are landing with parachutes and rapidly moving into formation to carry out military operations behind the enemy lines, while the deadly rain of 'chutes continues from the skies. Germany employed this technique in her recent drive against Warsaw.

WAR NEWS PICTURES

Keep a permanent record of the current war in Europe. Don't miss any of these important historical pictures. Copyright 1939, GUM, INC., Phila., Pa. Printed in U.S.A.

C-19-72

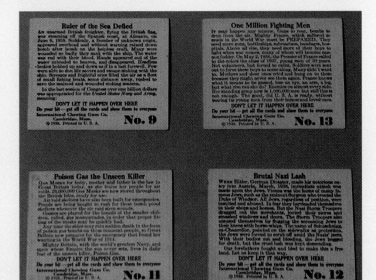

This set of bubble gum cards was produced in 1938 by the International Chewing Gum Company of Cambridge, Mass. Even in 1938, one year before the war started with the German invasion of Poland, American kids were being fed a steady diet of war scenarios. Card No. 12 depicts the brutal suppression of the Jews by the Nazis. This is the rarest of the non-sports cards of the late 1930s.

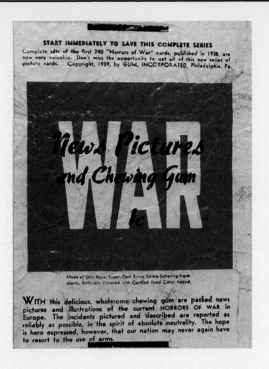

News Pictures and Chewing Gum

WAR

1¢

Made of Gum Base, Sugar, Corn Syrup, Edible Softening Ingredients. Artificially flavored with Certified Food Color Added.

WITH this delicious, wholesome chewing gum are packed news pictures and illustrations of the current HORRORS OF WAR in Europe. The incidents pictured and described are reported as reliably as possible, in the spirit of absolute neutrality. The hope is here expressed, however, that our nation may never again have to resort to the use of arms.

This 1939 Gum Inc. series of cards was produced just after the Germans invaded Poland, unleashing six years of war in Europe, Asia and North Africa and on the high seas.

56   German Junkers Bomber

The bombing of Polish cities by German planes is said to have given the "Ju-86K" an opportunity to test its effectiveness. Carrying a crew of five this bomber has a top speed of 242 miles per hour and a cruising range of over 1000 miles. The "Ju-86K" is provided with three gun turrets, one in the nose shielded by a sort of "birdcage" arrangement and two in back of the trailing edge of the wings, one above the fuselage and one below. The bombs (2200 lbs.) are carried within the plane.

WAR NEWS PICTURES

Keep a permanent record of the current war in Europe. Don't miss any of these important historical pictures. Copyright 1939, GUM, INC., Phila., Pa. Printed in U. S. A.

C-49-72

108   Warsaw's Sorrow

On October 25, 1939, two Americans who had just made a tour of the ruined city of Warsaw, gave a heart-rending account of the suffering they saw there. They estimated that 50,000 persons had been killed, hundreds of thousands injured and 35 per cent of the buildings destroyed! Thousands of victims of the famine are still being taken from the ruins. The worst famine is said to have occurred in the crowded tenements of the old city and in the Jewish quarter. Nazi welfare organizations now distribute hot meals and bread to Germans and Poles in the former capital, but the city's Jews, comprising about 30 per cent of the population, are said to have to live on their own resources.

WAR NEWS PICTURES

Keep a permanent record of the current war in Europe. Don't miss any of these important historical pictures. Copyright 1939, GUM, INC., Phila., Pa. Printed in U. S. A.

F-97-108

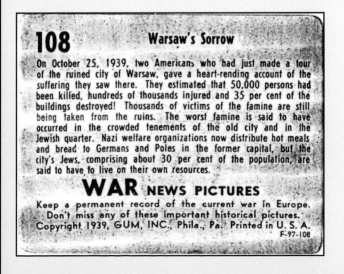

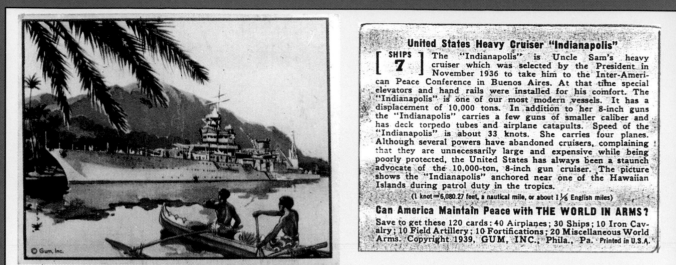

United States Heavy Cruiser "Indianapolis"

[SHIPS 7] The "Indianapolis" is Uncle Sam's heavy cruiser which was selected by the President in November 1936 to take him to the Inter-American Peace Conference in Buenos Aires. At that time special elevators and hand rails were installed for his comfort. The "Indianapolis" is one of our most modern vessels. It has a displacement of 10,000 tons. In addition to her 8-inch guns the "Indianapolis" carries a few guns of smaller caliber and has deck torpedo tubes and airplane catapults. Speed of the "Indianapolis" is about 33 knots. She carries four planes. Although several powers have abandoned cruisers, complaining that they are unnecessarily large and expensive while being poorly protected, the United States has always been a staunch advocate of the 10,000-ton, 8-inch gun cruiser. The picture shows the "Indianapolis" anchored near one of the Hawaiian Islands during patrol duty in the tropics.

(1 knot = 6,080.27 feet, a nautical mile, or about 1 1/6 English miles)

Can America Maintain Peace with THE WORLD IN ARMS?

Save to get these 120 cards: 40 Airplanes; 30 Ships; 10 Iron Cavalry; 10 Field Artillery; 10 Fortifications; 20 Miscellaneous World Arms. Copyright 1939, GUM, INC., Phila., Pa. Printed in U.S.A.

The cruiser *Indianapolis* carried the first atomic bomb to the island of Tinian in July 1945. On the way back to Hawaii it was attacked and sunk by a Japanese submarine with a great loss of life. This is one of 120 Gum Inc. cards. Notice the question--Can America Maintain Peace with the WORLD IN ARMS?

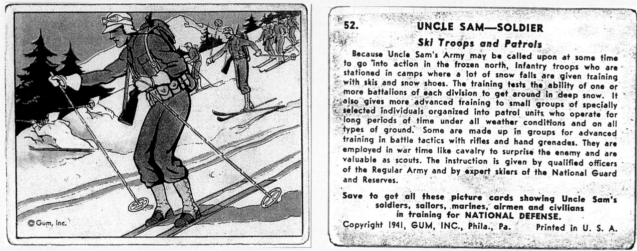

52. UNCLE SAM—SOLDIER

Ski Troops and Patrols

Because Uncle Sam's Army may be called upon at some time to go into action in the frozen north, infantry troops who are stationed in camps where a lot of snow falls are given training with skis and snow shoes. The training tests the ability of one or more battalions of each division to get around in deep snow. It also gives more advanced training to small groups of specially selected individuals organized into patrol units who operate for long periods of time under all weather conditions and on all types of ground. Some are made up in groups for advanced training in battle tactics with rifles and hand grenades. They are employed in war time like cavalry to surprise the enemy and are valuable as scouts. The instruction is given by qualified officers of the Regular Army and by expert skiers of the National Guard and Reserves.

Save to get all these picture cards showing Uncle Sam's soldiers, sailors, marines, airmen and civilians in training for NATIONAL DEFENSE.

Copyright 1941, GUM, INC., Phila., Pa.   Printed in U. S. A.

The 10th Mountain Division were the ski troops of the US Army and trained at Camp Hale, high in the Colorado Rockies. They did not see action (except for a brief tour in the Aleutians) until early 1945 when they fought vicious battles in the Northern Italian campaign. After the war many of its members went into the ski business across the United States.

92. Navy Task Force Cripples Japs in Aleutians

The silence about the Japs in the fog-bound Aleutians was finally broken by a Naval Report on August 11, 1942, showing that the Army and Navy had been in action during July and August, attacking enemy shore installations. On August 8, a task force of the Pacific fleet, protected by Navy patrol planes, heavily bombarded enemy ships, camp facilities and shore installations at Kiska. The attack was a complete surprise. The enemy mistaking the first salvos of shells for air bombs opened fire with anti-aircraft batteries on imaginary planes. The intense bombardment from our destroyer and cruiser guns soon silenced these shore batteries. On August 9, Navy patrol planes followed up the bombardment by attacking two cargo ships in Kiska Harbor.

This is one of a series of educational cards which come wrapped in packages of War Gum. Save to complete your collection.

Copyright 1942, GUM, INC., Phila., Pa.   Printed in U. S. A.

Buy War Bonds and Stamps for VICTORY

The Aleutian campaign was a little known theater of war in Alaska and the only North American territory occupied by the enemy during the war. The Japanese took over two islands in the Aleutian chain in June 1942 and were expelled from them in May and July 1943.

General Douglas MacArthur

Without a doubt the American general with the best PR department was General Douglas MacArthur, commander of Allied forces in the southwest Pacific. After escaping from the Philippines in early 1942 he led his forces to victory after victory and directed the occupation of Japan after the war. His name and face were everywhere in the United States.

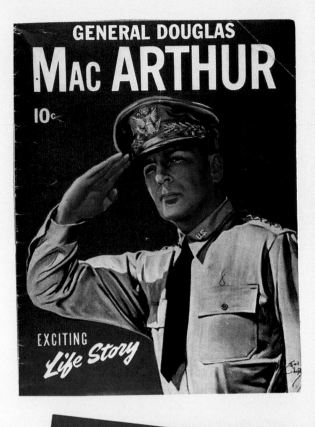

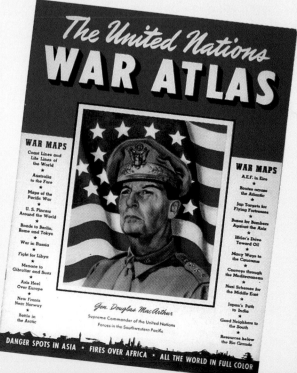

Matchbook Covers and
Tobacco Products

    One of the best advertising tools on the home front was the matchbook. Millions were distributed with a compact ad format with color images to enhance the national team effort to win the war. Everytime a match was struck, American's were reminded to save scrap, buy war bonds and keep their lips sealed.

    Matchbooks had patriotic themes and often had pin-up girls who were referred to as "Wartime Maidens." They posed seductively, straddled bombs and had slogans printed on them such as "You buy 'Em, We'll fly 'Em, Kick 'Em in the Axis, Remember Pearl Harbor, Don't Talk Chum, Chew Topp's Gum" and V for Victory." Other covers were adorned with military ships, planes, tanks, bases and clubs.

During the war, cigarettes were used as a form of money in many theaters of action. They were passed out at canteens, USO Clubs and even packed in parcels sent to prisoners-of-war. These were some of the most popular brands.

Punch Boards

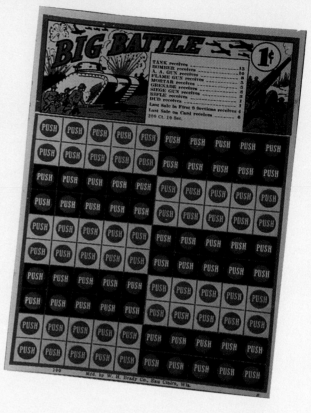

Punch boards were very popular during the war and were produced in a variety of forms.

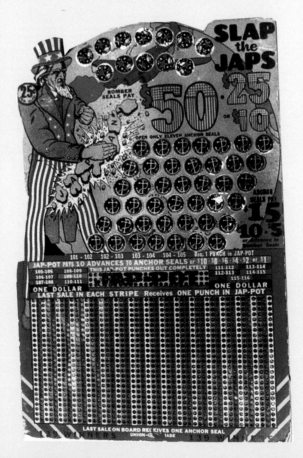

Not only was Rosie the Riveter very popular but so was her sister.

Cinderellas

PROPAGANDA WAR STICKERS were produced by the government and illustrated paintings and political messages were aimed at the American public. Saving scrap metal and fat, recruiting men and women into the Armed Forces, planting victory gardens, conserving food, fuel oil, tin cans and rubber and war bond financing were a few of the topics the stickers covered.

This large, rare, coin operated game was produced for retail outlets. It took one penny to poison Hitler. It is a prime example of the lengths to which people would go to portray Hitler and the Nazis as evil.

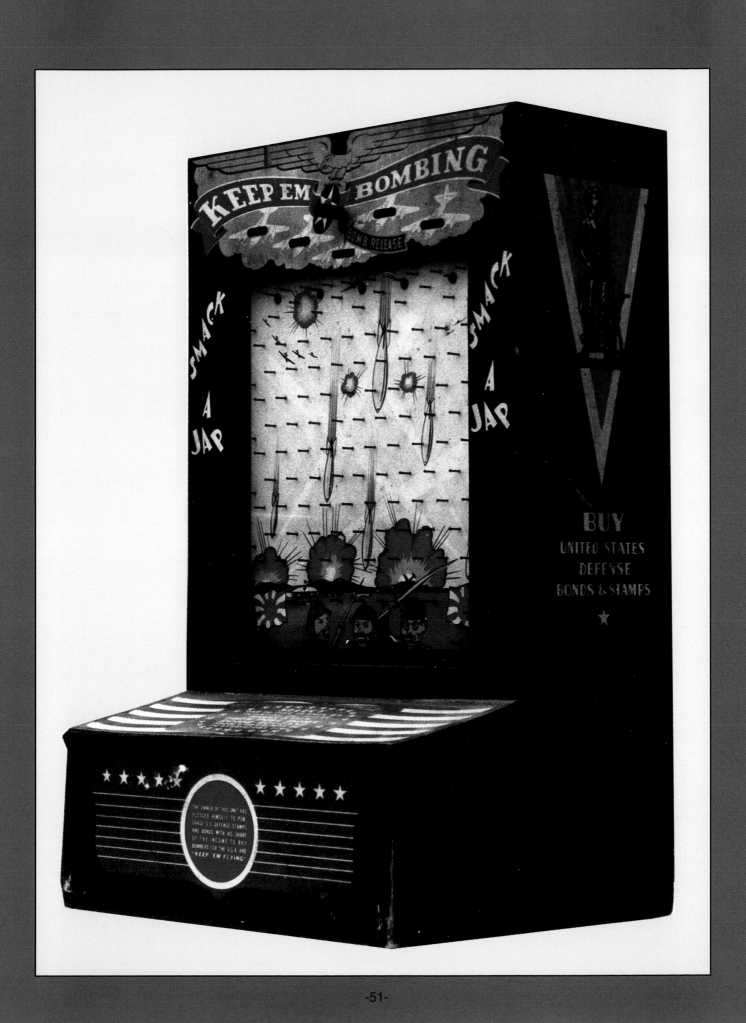

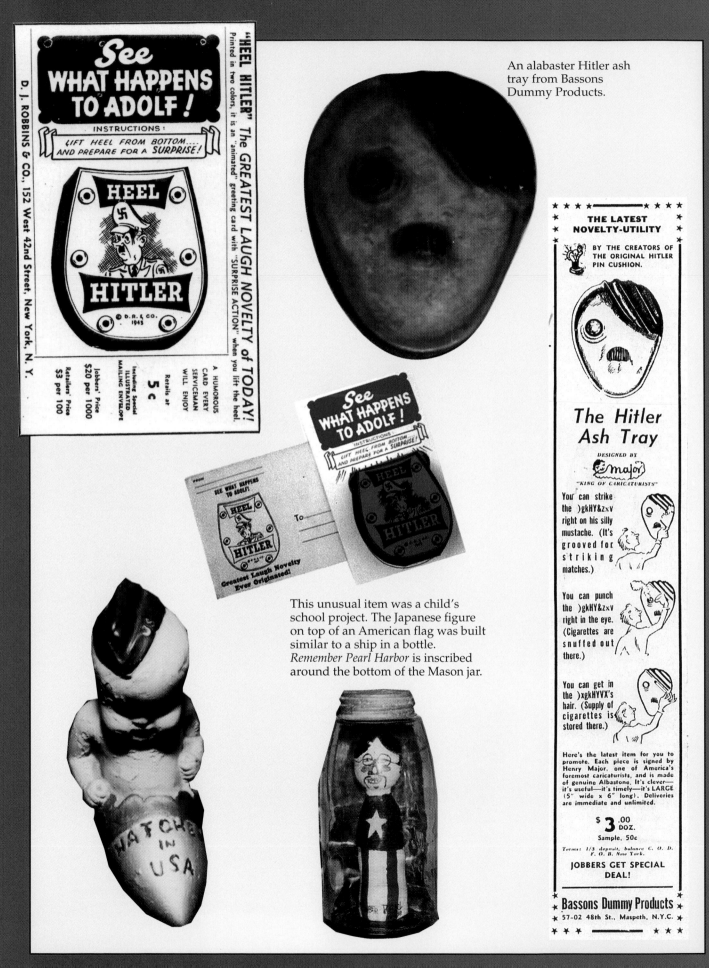

An alabaster Hitler ash tray from Bassons Dummy Products.

This unusual item was a child's school project. The Japanese figure on top of an American flag was built similar to a ship in a bottle. *Remember Pearl Harbor* is inscribed around the bottom of the Mason jar.

THE NEW DESTROYER BANK
BLAST THE AXIS

THE NEW DESTROYER BANK
Retails for
69c

A STREAMLINED replica of America's symbol of armored might, the DESTROYER BANK stands as a constant reminder that we must continue saving our pennies, nickels, dimes and quarters to buy the real thing to BLAST THE AXIS towards VICTORY . . .

SPECIFICATIONS

✓ 5 inches in height—3½ inches in width—11 inches in length.
✓ Baked finish in United States Navy regulation Battleship grey.
✓ Individually boxed—36 to shipping carton—weight 40 lbs.
✓ Attractive red, white and blue label adds to patriotic motive and display appeal.
✓ Eight sales compelling window streamers in each carton.
✓ Made of strong plaster, it has utility for both ornamental and savings.

SOLD THROUGH JOBBERS ONLY

NOVELTY MANUFACTURING CO. • 71 WEST 23rd STREET • **NEW YORK CITY**
CHICAGO OFFICE—1234 MERCHANDISE MART

A bomb bank.

THE NEW SENSATIONAL TANK BANK
BLAST THE AXIS

THE NEW TANK BANK
Retails for
50c

A STREAMLINED replica of America's symbol of armored might, the TANK BANK stands as a constant reminder that we must continue saving our pennies, nickels, dimes and quarters to buy the real thing to BLAST THE AXIS towards VICTORY . . .

SPECIFICATIONS

✓ 5 inches in height—3 inches in width—8 inches in length.
✓ Baked finish in United States Army regulation olive drab.
✓ Individually boxed—48 to shipping carton—weight 48 lbs.
✓ Attractive red, white and blue label adds to patriotic motive and display appeal.
✓ Eight sales compelling window streamers in each carton.
✓ Made of strong plastic composition, it has utility for both ornamental and savings.

SOLD THROUGH JOBBERS ONLY

NOVELTY MANUFACTURING CO. • 71 WEST 23rd STREET • **NEW YORK CITY**
CHICAGO OFFICE—1234 MERCHANDISE MART

This sales point of purchase for Double Kay nuts is applicable to the three characters shown. However, this is unusual as it shows Hitler, Mussolini and Stalin. This board must be dated from late 1939 through mid 1941 before America entered the war and became an ally of Russia.

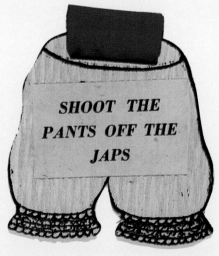

Many different pin cushion figurines were made during the war of Hitler, Tojo and Mussolini.

A sewing kit with Mussolini on one side and Hitler on the other. Pins were stuck in their behinds.

The three Axis leaders were portrayed in these porcelain ash trays with their original tags. These are very rare items especially with the tags intact.

This ash tray set is a little different than the one above and lays flat rather than upright.

A very rare Adolf piggy bank and its original box.

A wood and paper pull toy, an American soldier kicking a Nazi.

UNCLE SAM'S PEACE TERMS

A chalk plaque.

This set is one of the rarest anti-Axis items in existence. One could really "take it out" on the Axis leaders with their bowling ball.

This chalkware figurine is captioned, "I Got My Jap."

A large chamber pot from The Morning Call Company of Wheeling, West Virginia. Hitler's caricature has been painted on the inside bottom.

The standard party game, "Pin the Tail on the Donkey," was modified several times to fit public sentiment.

A candy box.

A one-dimensional dog house expounding the problem of worker absenteeism.

These figures are approximately seven inches tall. They are part of the Young Patriot set.

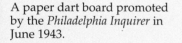

A paper dart board promoted by the *Philadelphia Inquirer* in June 1943.

X-RAY PHOTO OF *Hitler's* BRAIN

How good a Phrenologist are you? Can you tell what each object in Hitler's head denotes? If not, see other side.

© 1942 B. F. LONG

X-RAY PHOTO of *Hitler's* BRAIN

INSANE

WE ARE THE SUPERIOR RACE

AXIS SERIES NO. 51

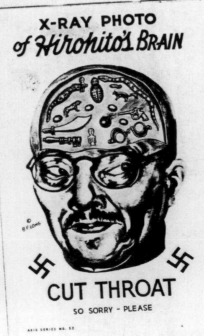

X-RAY PHOTO of *Hirohito's* BRAIN

CUT THROAT

SO SORRY - PLEASE

AXIS SERIES NO. 52

X-RAY PHOTO of *Mussolini's* BRAIN

DUNCE

SAYS. *The* ALLIES MAKE ME SO MAD THAT I AM GOING RIGHT OUT IN THE BACK YARD AND EAT WORMS.

AXIS SERIES NO. 53

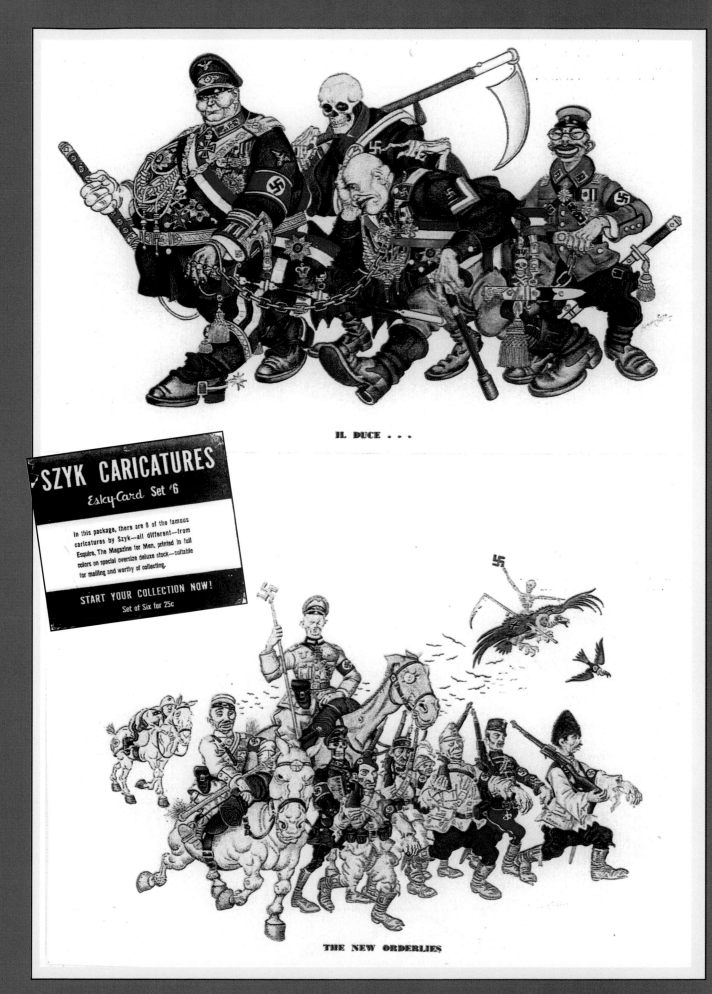

IL DUCE . . .

THE NEW ORDERLIES

COWARD
APR
20
P.M.
1943
S.C.

This cover commemorates the noble birth of Adolf Hitler (born Adolf Schickelgruber). Reproduced above is a quaint photograph of the German Fuehrer at the tender age of sixteen. The universe has been immeasurably blessed by the merciful deeds of this compassionate man. He was born in Austria on April 20th, 1889. May his soul rest in peace (soon).

John E. Williams,
2031 Green Ridge St.,
Dunmore, Pa.

D. J. Robbins "slams the axis" with postcards

Something new is being offered by D. Robbins & Co. of New York City, in "Slam the Axis" post cards. The well known artist, Joe Gross has created for D. Robbins & Co., 152 West 52nd street, New York, a series of 6 clever drawings, all of a humorous nature, which are being printed in standard post card size. The cards will retail at 6 for 10c; are packed 6 different subjects in a "self mailing" envelope, and 50 of these cards to the boys in the Service." Also "a laugh in every card."

The retailer earns 40% profit when selling the cards at 6 for 10c and a still greater profit by selling them at 2c each. Printed from the fine half-tone engravings, they compare favorably with similar quality cards that usually retail at 5c each. D. Robbins & Co. state that advance orders placed by jobbers, distributors and chain stores indicate sales of "Slam The Axis" cards will be tremendous. Deliveries are now being made.

envelopes in an attractive counter display box. Featured on the display box is the wording "Mail a set

FORTUNE TELLER:
"I SEE A BAD FINISH FOR YOU RATS"

HICKORY GAP
GOES TO WAR
BY
Paul Webb

U.S. NAVY FIGHTER
GRUMMAN F4F-3
OVER 350 M.P.H.

NEW "WAR BABY"
BREAKING ALL RECORDS
FOR QUICK PROFITS

SOCK THE JAPS WAR BOND BANK

Retails for 25c. Large size. Finished in three colors for attention-getting sales appeal. A "Natural" to tie-in with current War Bond drives. Holds $18.75 in pennies, nickels, dimes, quarters, half dollars. When full bank is broken and savings used to buy War Bonds. Just the item to break the after-Christmas slump. Every member of the family will want one. It's timely, patriotic, practical. Not a toy but a substantial well made item that looks the price and more! Get on the profit bond wagon with the Bond Bank that has everything!

IMMEDIATE DELIVERY—ANY QUANTITY

You can promote this item to the hilt without any delivery worries. Made of non-essential materials. Big volume production means prompt action on orders. Orders shipped same day received.

LOW SHIPPING COST—NO BREAKAGE

Made of improved fibrous material that eliminates loss from breakage. Light weight saves shipping costs. Packed 72 to a carton.

RUSH ORDER OR SEND FOR SAMPLE

The quicker you get it on your counter the sooner your profits start. Write or wire today. Sample sent to rated firms if desired.

FREE
DISPLAY
MATERIAL
IN COLOR

25¢

LITE PRODUCTS CO.

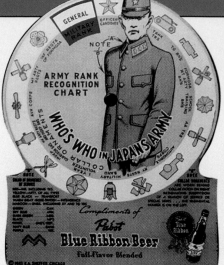

This is a very unusual piece. The firecrackers were made in China during the war, Tojo, Hilter and Mossolini (notice the name spelling) on the cover. But China was occupied by the Japanese and there was no access to the country for many years except by air over the "Hump" to India. Were these firecrackers brought out by plane and where were they made in China?

The five sons of Mr. and Mrs. Thomas E. Sullivan of Waterloo, Iowa were killed aboard the *USS Juneau* on November 14, 1942 in the Guadalcanal area. After this tragedy, the US Government did not allow brothers to serve on the same ship.

Show the World

YOU'RE PROUD OF YOUR BOY IN SERVICE!

10¢

FAST COLOR

SWEETHEART! WIFE! MOTHER! DAD! SISTER! Wear this Badge of Service Proudly

CARELESS MATCHES AID THE AXIS!

PREVENT FOREST FIRES

A SLIP OF THE LIP MIGHT SINK A SHIP

DON'T DISCUSS MILITARY INFORMATION

EASTMAN S. F. NO. 450

The vast forests of the Pacific Northwest were a tempting target for the Japanese to start forest fires. Late in the war thousands of incendiary balloon bombs were launched from Japan and carried by wind currents to the United States. Fortunately none of the balloon bombs started any fires, but five persons were killed in Oregon when they discovered one on the ground and it blew up.

DON'T BE A SAP . . . . KEEP CLOSED THAT GAP THAT'S IN YOUR TRAP AND THEN WE'LL SLAP THE TREACHEROUS JAP CLEAR OFF THE MAP

EASTMAN S. F. NO. 451

MADE IN JAPAN

CAUGHT IN THE PACIFIC

TANNED IN THE U.S.A.

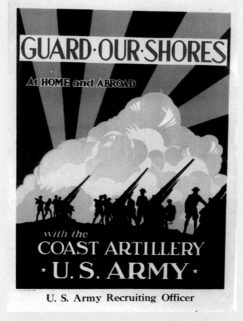

GUARD·OUR·SHORES

At HOME and ABROAD

with the COAST ARTILLERY · U.S. ARMY ·

U. S. Army Recruiting Officer

OUR CARELESSNESS Their Secret Weapon

PREVENT FOREST FIRES

U. S. Dept. of Agriculture—Forest Service State of New Hampshire Forestry & Recreation Dept.

HUNTING LICENSE

ISSUED TO _____

— OPEN SEASON —
FOR THAT VILE STINKING VIPER KNOWN AS
JAP-SNAKE
Will be recognized by that hissing S-S-S
noise that sounds like "SO SORRY PLEASE"
WARNING - Do not turn your back, as this
animal is noted for Back Stabbing !
Signed—Viper Exterminating Society.

© 1942 JOKERR Nov. N.Y.

DUPLICATE—MEMO, EXHIBITOR'S COPY

Victory Pledge Agreement

I PLEDGE MY SCREEN
to the showing of
VICTORY FEATURETTES

Rio Theater,
Jordon, Montana.

As a part of my contribution to America's war effort in co-operation with all branches
of the Motion Picture Industry of the United States, and in co-operation with Universal,
which has agreed to produce and distribute 4 Victory Featurettes to aid this country's fight
for freedom, I hereby agree to contract for and play these Featurettes when and as they be-
come available for my theatre and to pay for each Victory Featurette on the following terms:

4 VICTORY FEATURETTES	No. days: 2-3	Rental terms: $2.00

It is mutually understood and agreed that our regular license agreement covering the
licensing of Featurettes or Short Subject motion pictures now in use by us shall cover the
licensing of the herein mentioned Victory Featurettes. It is further understood that no
specific run is licensed or any clearance granted. Universal, on its part, and in co-
operation with the U. S. Government's Motion Picture Division, agrees that a print of
each Victory Featurette will be delivered to you when and as it becomes available for
your use.

Universal also agrees to turn over all profits derived from these Victory Featurettes
to a war-effort fund to be designated. We are proud to share this privilege with you.

Agreed to: Universal Pictures Co., Inc.
Retain this copy for your files.

_____   _____
Exhibitor   Vice-President

Universal Film Exchanges, Inc.
Bruce Loveless
Salesman.   Date December 29, 1942

V . . . —

Civilian Defense

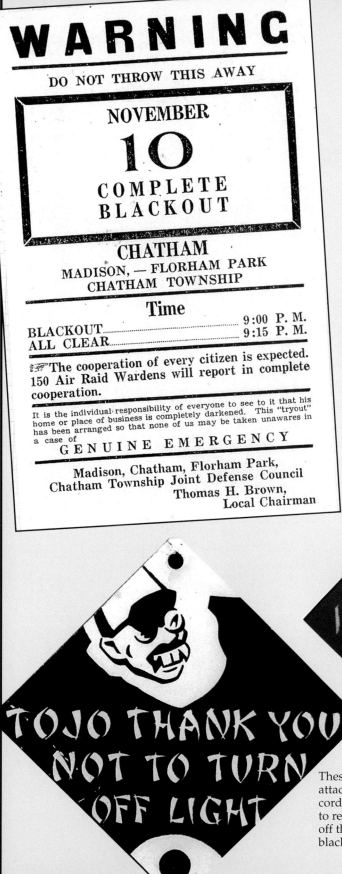

DO NOT THROW THIS AWAY

NOVEMBER
10
COMPLETE
BLACKOUT

CHATHAM

MADISON, — FLORHAM PARK
CHATHAM TOWNSHIP

Time

BLACKOUT...9:00 P. M.
ALL CLEAR...9:15 P. M.

☞ The cooperation of every citizen is expected. 150 Air Raid Wardens will report in complete cooperation.

It is the individual responsibility of everyone to see to it that his home or place of business is completely darkened. This "tryout" has been arranged so that none of us may be taken unawares in a case of GENUINE EMERGENCY

Madison, Chatham, Florham Park, Chatham Township Joint Defense Council
Thomas H. Brown, Local Chairman

Hundreds of uses for
BLACKOUT ★ KUTOUTS
THE NEW WONDER MATERIAL
Glows in the dark

FOR FUN   FOR UTILITY   FOR THE BLACKOUT

PRACTICAL • INSTRUCTIVE • MYSTIFYING • FUN

TOJO THANK YOU NOT TO TURN OFF LIGHT

It gifts a pleasure for you to leave light burn

These cards were attached to the pull cord of a light fixture to remind one to turn off the lights during a blackout.

Spotting Enemy Planes

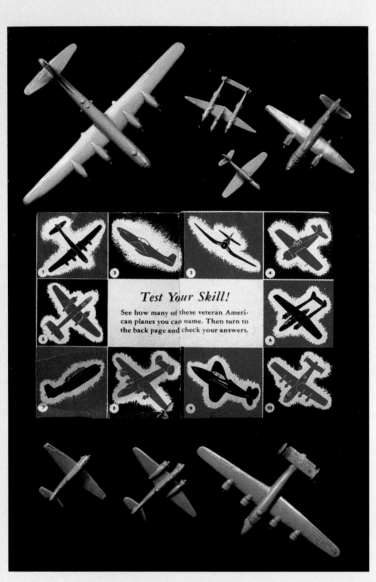

Test Your Skill!

See how many of these veteran American planes you can name. Then turn to the back page and check your answers.

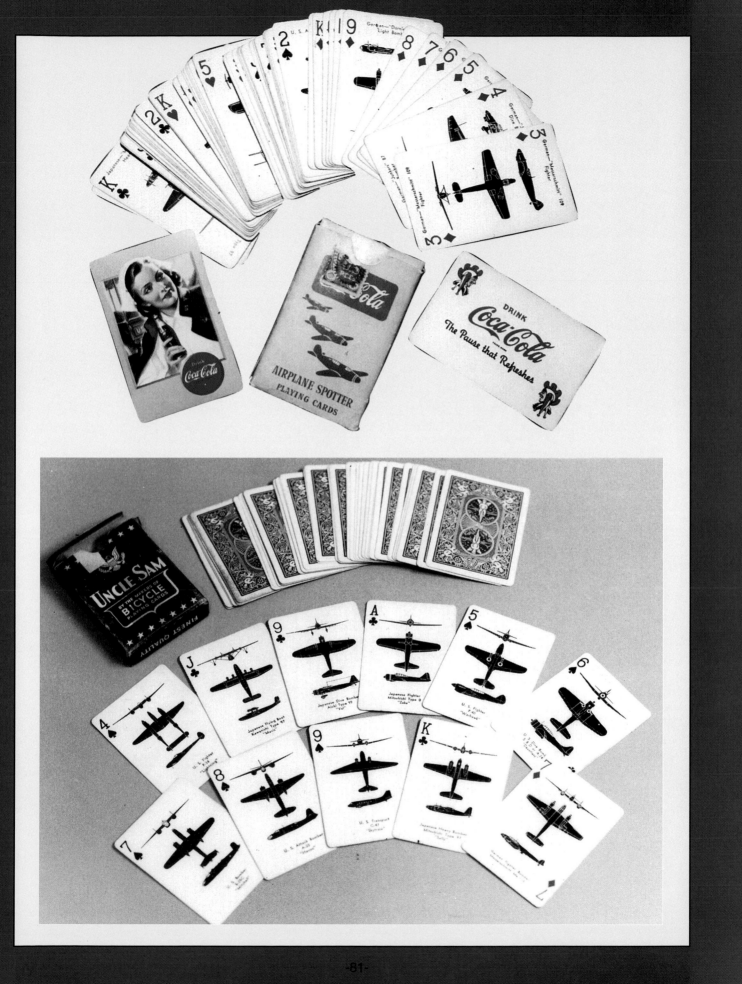

Reed Associates' popular punch-out set of famous Allied fighting planes, "3 Flying Models," also contained "American Ace Spotter," a rotating dial made of paper with forty-eight plane silhouettes. The 1944 issue date indicates the continuing popularity of spotter ID toys long after public fear of enemy air raids had dissipated.

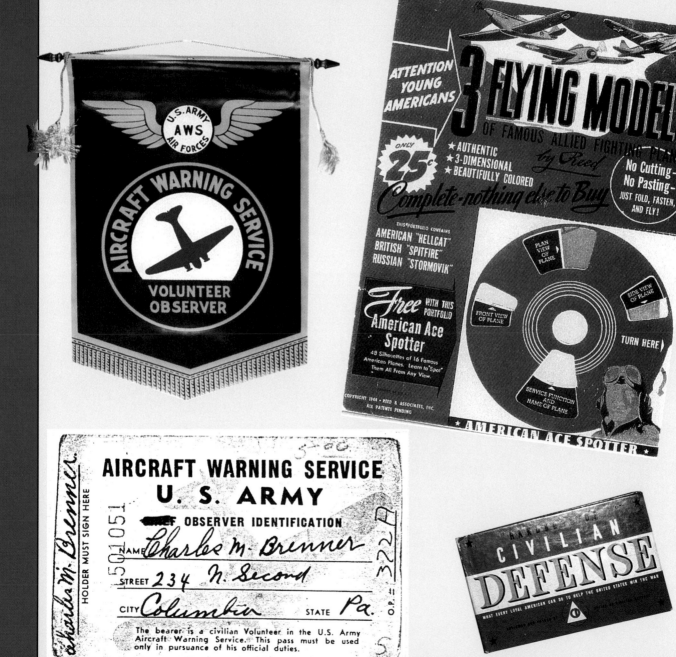

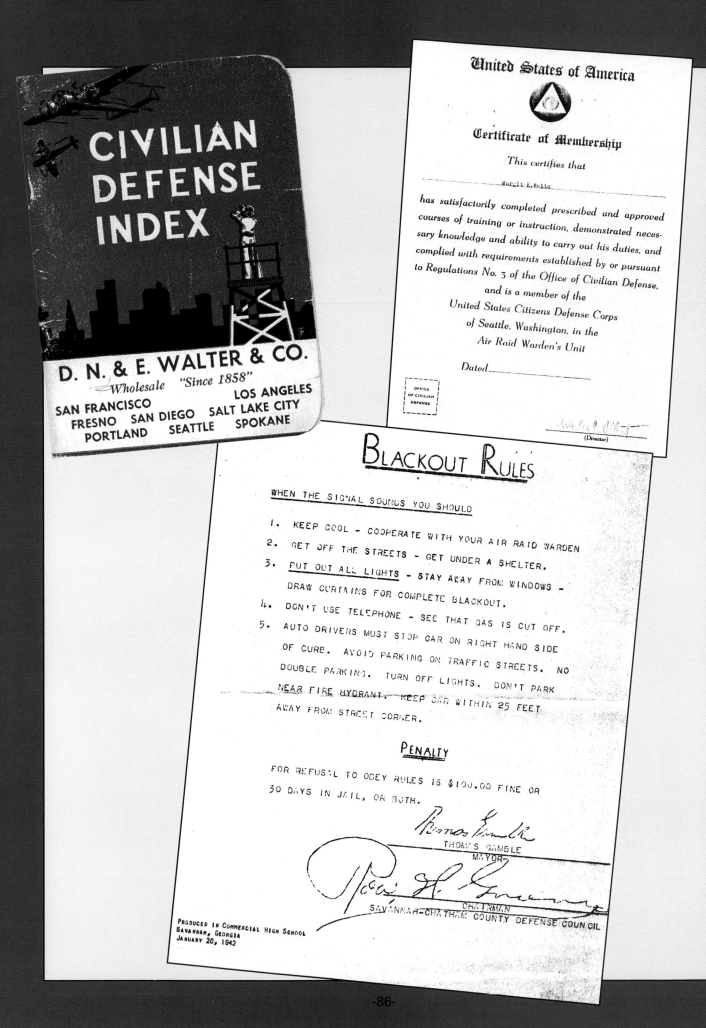

CIVILIAN DEFENSE INDEX

D. N. & E. WALTER & CO.

Wholesale "Since 1858"

SAN FRANCISCO   LOS ANGELES
FRESNO   SAN DIEGO   SALT LAKE CITY
PORTLAND   SEATTLE   SPOKANE

United States of America

Certificate of Membership

This certifies that

Marell E. Watts

has satisfactorily completed prescribed and approved courses of training or instruction, demonstrated necessary knowledge and ability to carry out his duties, and complied with requirements established by or pursuant to Regulations No. 3 of the Office of Civilian Defense, and is a member of the

United States Citizens Defense Corps
of Seattle, Washington, in the
Air Raid Warden's Unit

Dated _____

OFFICE
OF CIVILIAN
DEFENSE

_____
(Director)

BLACKOUT RULES

WHEN THE SIGNAL SOUNDS YOU SHOULD

1. KEEP COOL - COOPERATE WITH YOUR AIR RAID WARDEN

2. GET OFF THE STREETS - GET UNDER A SHELTER.

3. PUT OUT ALL LIGHTS - STAY AWAY FROM WINDOWS - DRAW CURTAINS FOR COMPLETE BLACKOUT.

4. DON'T USE TELEPHONE - SEE THAT GAS IS CUT OFF.

5. AUTO DRIVERS MUST STOP CAR ON RIGHT HAND SIDE OF CURB. AVOID PARKING ON TRAFFIC STREETS. NO DOUBLE PARKING. TURN OFF LIGHTS. DON'T PARK NEAR FIRE HYDRANT. KEEP CAR WITHIN 25 FEET AWAY FROM STREET CORNER.

PENALTY

FOR REFUSAL TO OBEY RULES IS $100.00 FINE OR 30 DAYS IN JAIL, OR BOTH.

THOMAS GAMBLE
MAYOR

CHAIRMAN
SAVANNAH-CHATHAM COUNTY DEFENSE COUNCIL

PRODUCED IN COMMERCIAL HIGH SCHOOL
SAVANNAH, GEORGIA
JANUARY 20, 1942

Music and Movies
of the War

Like Vera Lynn in England, Kate Smith was the American songster during the war years.

The Movies

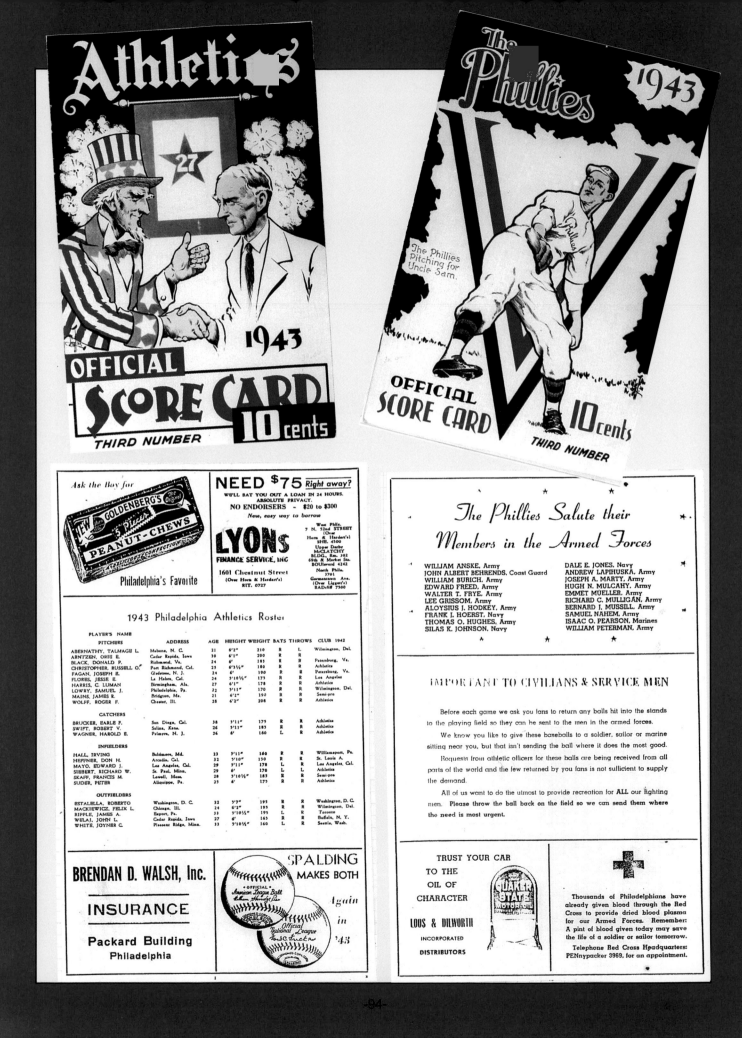

The Phillies Salute their Members in the Armed Forces

WILLIAM ANSKE, Army
JOHN ALBERT BEHRENDS, Coast Guard
WILLIAM BURICH, Army
EDWARD FREED, Army
WALTER T. FRYE, Army
LEE GRISSOM, Army
ALOYSIUS J. HODKEY, Army
FRANK J. HOERST, Navy
THOMAS O. HUGHES, Army
SILAS K. JOHNSON, Navy

DALE E. JONES, Navy
ANDREW LAPIHUSKA, Army
JOSEPH A. MARTY, Army
HUGH N. MULCAHY, Army
EMMET MUELLER, Army
RICHARD C. MULLIGAN, Army
BERNARD J. MUSSILL, Army
SAMUEL NAHEM, Army
ISAAC O. PEARSON, Marines
WILLIAM PETERMAN, Army

IMPORTANT TO CIVILIANS & SERVICE MEN

Before each game we ask you fans to return any balls hit into the stands to the playing field so they can be sent to the men in the armed forces.

We know you like to give these baseballs to a soldier, sailor or marine sitting near you, but that isn't sending the ball where it does the most good.

Requests from athletic officers for these balls are being received from all parts of the world and the few returned by you fans is not sufficient to supply the demand.

All of us want to do the utmost to provide recreation for ALL our fighting men. Please throw the ball back on the field so we can send them where the need is most urgent.

1943 Philadelphia Athletics Roster

PLAYER'S NAME	ADDRESS	AGE	HEIGHT	WEIGHT	BATS	THROWS	CLUB 1942
PITCHERS							
ABERNATHY, TALMAGE L.	Mebane, N. C.	21	6'2"	210	R	L	Wilmington, Del.
ARNTZEN, ORIE E.	Cedar Rapids, Iowa	30	6'1"	200	R	R	Petersburg, Va.
BLACK, DONALD P.	Richmond, Va.	24	6'	185	R	R	Athletics
CHRISTOPHER, RUSSELL O.	Port Richmond, Cal.	25	6'1½"	180	R	R	Petersburg, Va.
FAGAN, JOSEPH B.	Gladstone, N. J.	24	6'	190	R	R	
FLORES, JESSE E.	La Habra, Cal.	24	5'10½"	175	R	R	Los Angeles
HARRIS, C. LUMAN	Birmingham, Ala.	27	6'1"	178	R	R	Athletics
LOWRY, SAMUEL J.	Philadelphia, Pa.	22	5'11"	170	R	R	Wilmington, Del.
MAINS, JAMES R.	Bridgton, Me.	21	6'2"	190	R	R	Semi-pro
WOLFF, ROGER F.	Chester, Ill.	28	6'2"	208	R	R	Athletics
CATCHERS							
BRUCKER, EARLE F.	San Diego, Cal.	38	5'11"	175	R	R	Athletics
SWIFT, ROBERT V.	Salina, Kans.	26	5'11"	185	R	R	Athletics
WAGNER, HAROLD E.	Palmyra, N. J.	26	6'	160	L	R	Athletics
INFIELDERS							
HALL, IRVING	Baltimore, Md.	23	5'11"	160	R	R	Williamsport, Pa.
HEFFNER, DON H.	Arcadia, Cal.	32	5'10"	150	R	R	St. Louis A.
MAYO, EDWARD J.	Los Angeles, Cal.	29	5'11"	178	L	R	Los Angeles, Cal.
SIEBERT, RICHARD W.	St. Paul, Minn.	29	6'	178	L	L	Athletics
SKAFF, FRANCIS M.	Lowell, Mass.	28	5'10½"	185	R	R	Semi-pro
SUDER, PETER	Aliquippa, Pa.	25	6'	175	R	R	Athletics
OUTFIELDERS							
ESTALELLA, ROBERTO	Washington, D. C.	32	5'7"	195	R	R	Washington, D. C.
MACKIEWICZ, FELIX L.	Chicago, Ill.	24	6'2"	195	L	R	Wilmington, Del.
RIPPLE, JAMES A.	Export, Pa.	33	5'10½"	195	L	R	Toronto
WELAJ, JOHN L.	Cedar Rapids, Iowa	27	6'	165	R	R	Buffalo, N. Y.
WHITE, JOYNER C.	Pleasant Ridge, Minn.	33	5'10½"	160	L	R	Seattle, Wash.

Stage Door Canteen

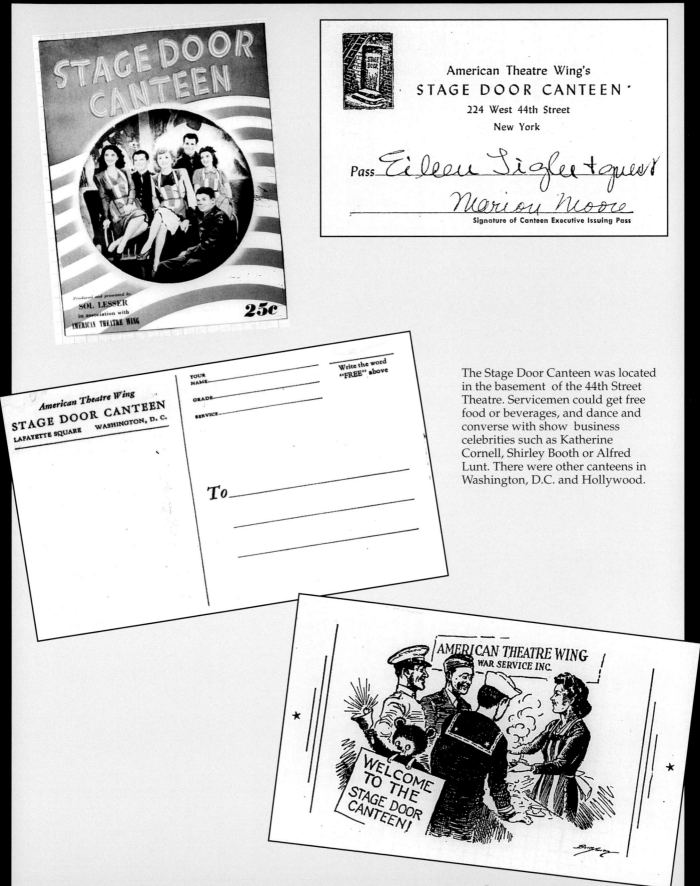

American Theatre Wing's
STAGE DOOR CANTEEN
224 West 44th Street
New York

Pass _Eileen Sigler + guest_

Marion Moore

Signature of Canteen Executive Issuing Pass

American Theatre Wing
STAGE DOOR CANTEEN
LAFAYETTE SQUARE   WASHINGTON, D. C.

YOUR NAME
GRADE
SERVICE

Write the word "FREE" above

To

The Stage Door Canteen was located in the basement of the 44th Street Theatre. Servicemen could get free food or beverages, and dance and converse with show business celebrities such as Katherine Cornell, Shirley Booth or Alfred Lunt. There were other canteens in Washington, D.C. and Hollywood.

AMERICAN THEATRE WING
WAR SERVICE INC.

WELCOME TO THE STAGE DOOR CANTEEN!

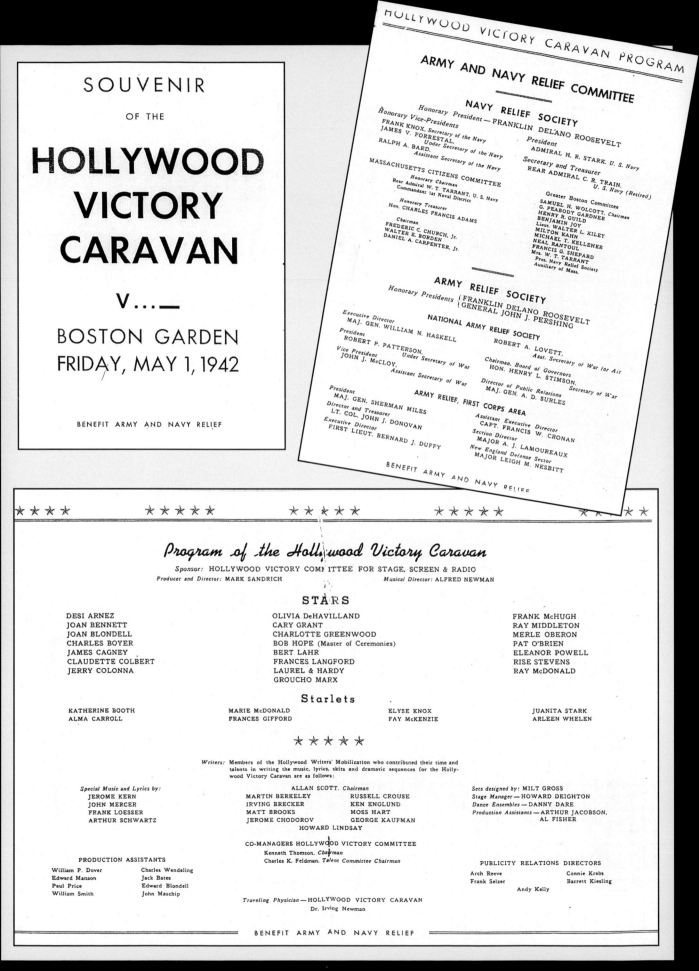

SOUVENIR

OF THE

HOLLYWOOD VICTORY CARAVAN

V...—

BOSTON GARDEN
FRIDAY, MAY 1, 1942

BENEFIT ARMY AND NAVY RELIEF

HOLLYWOOD VICTORY CARAVAN PROGRAM

ARMY AND NAVY RELIEF COMMITTEE

NAVY RELIEF SOCIETY

Honorary President — FRANKLIN DELANO ROOSEVELT
Honorary Vice-Presidents
FRANK KNOX, Secretary of the Navy
JAMES V. FORRESTAL, Under Secretary of the Navy
RALPH A. BARD, Assistant Secretary of the Navy

President
ADMIRAL H. R. STARK, U. S. Navy
Secretary and Treasurer
REAR ADMIRAL C. R. TRAIN, U. S. Navy (Retired)

MASSACHUSETTS CITIZENS COMMITTEE
Honorary Chairman
Rear Admiral W. T. TARRANT, U. S. Navy
Commandant 1st Naval District
Honorary Treasurer
Hon. CHARLES FRANCIS ADAMS
Chairman
FREDERIC C. CHURCH, Jr.
WALTER E. BORDEN
DANIEL A. CARPENTER, Jr.

Greater Boston Committee
SAMUEL H. WOLCOTT, Chairman
G. PEABODY GARDNER
HENRY R. GUILD
BENJAMIN JOY
Lieut. WALTER L. KILEY
MILTON KAHN
MICHAEL T. KELLEHER
NEAL RANTOUL
FRANCIS G. SHEPARD
Mrs. W. T. TARRANT
Pres. Navy Relief Society
Auxiliary of Mass.

ARMY RELIEF SOCIETY

Honorary Presidents {FRANKLIN DELANO ROOSEVELT
{GENERAL JOHN J. PERSHING

NATIONAL ARMY RELIEF SOCIETY
Executive Director
MAJ. GEN. WILLIAM N. HASKELL
President
ROBERT P. PATTERSON, Under Secretary of War
Vice President
JOHN J. McCLOY, Assistant Secretary of War

ROBERT A. LOVETT, Asst. Secretary of War for Air
Chairman, Board of Governors
HON. HENRY L. STIMSON, Secretary of War
Director of Public Relations
MAJ. GEN. A. D. SURLES

ARMY RELIEF, FIRST CORPS AREA
President
MAJ. GEN. SHERMAN MILES
Director and Treasurer
LT. COL. JOHN J. DONOVAN
Executive Director
FIRST LIEUT. BERNARD J. DUFFY

Assistant Executive Director
CAPT. FRANCIS W. CRONAN
Section Director
MAJOR A. J. LAMOUREAUX
New England Defense Sector
MAJOR LEIGH M. NESBITT

BENEFIT ARMY AND NAVY RELIEF

★★★★ ★★★★★ ★★★★★ ★★★★★ ★★★★★

Program of the Hollywood Victory Caravan

Sponsor: HOLLYWOOD VICTORY COMMITTEE FOR STAGE, SCREEN & RADIO
Producer and Director: MARK SANDRICH   *Musical Director:* ALFRED NEWMAN

STARS

DESI ARNEZ
JOAN BENNETT
JOAN BLONDELL
CHARLES BOYER
JAMES CAGNEY
CLAUDETTE COLBERT
JERRY COLONNA

OLIVIA DeHAVILLAND
CARY GRANT
CHARLOTTE GREENWOOD
BOB HOPE (Master of Ceremonies)
BERT LAHR
FRANCES LANGFORD
LAUREL & HARDY
GROUCHO MARX

FRANK McHUGH
RAY MIDDLETON
MERLE OBERON
PAT O'BRIEN
ELEANOR POWELL
RISE STEVENS
RAY McDONALD

Starlets

KATHERINE BOOTH
ALMA CARROLL

MARIE McDONALD
FRANCES GIFFORD

ELYSE KNOX
FAY McKENZIE

JUANITA STARK
ARLEEN WHELEN

★★★★★

Writers: Members of the Hollywood Writers' Mobilization who contributed their time and talents in writing the music, lyrics, skits and dramatic sequences for the Hollywood Victory Caravan are as follows:

Special Music and Lyrics by:
JEROME KERN
JOHN MERCER
FRANK LOESSER
ARTHUR SCHWARTZ

ALLAN SCOTT, *Chairman*
MARTIN BERKELEY   RUSSELL CROUSE
IRVING BRECKER   KEN ENGLUND
MATT BROOKS   MOSS HART
JEROME CHODOROV   GEORGE KAUFMAN
HOWARD LINDSAY

Sets designed by: MILT GROSS
Stage Manager — HOWARD DEIGHTON
Dance Ensembles — DANNY DARE
Production Assistants — ARTHUR JACOBSON,
AL FISHER

CO-MANAGERS HOLLYWOOD VICTORY COMMITTEE
Kenneth Thomson, *Chairman*
Charles K. Feldman, *Talent Committee Chairman*

PRODUCTION ASSISTANTS
William P. Dover   Charles Wendeling
Edward Manson   Jack Bates
Paul Price   Edward Blondell
William Smith   John Maschip

PUBLICITY RELATIONS DIRECTORS
Arch Reeve   Connie Krebs
Frank Selzer   Barrett Kiesling
Andy Kelly

Traveling Physician — HOLLYWOOD VICTORY CARAVAN
Dr. Irving Newman

BENEFIT ARMY AND NAVY RELIEF

Joan Blondell

Jerry Colonna

Claudette

Pat O'Brien

Eleanor Powell

Ray McDonald

BENEFIT ARMY AND NAVY RELIEF

War related exhibits were held in large and small cities throughout the United States to promote patriotism and war bond sales.

The Nation's Magazines
Go to War

"The Dictator" starring Charlie Chaplin was a famous parody of Hitler produced in 1940.

This issue is dated December 13, 1941, six days after the Pearl Harbor attack. President Roosevelt would lead the nation until his death in April 1945.

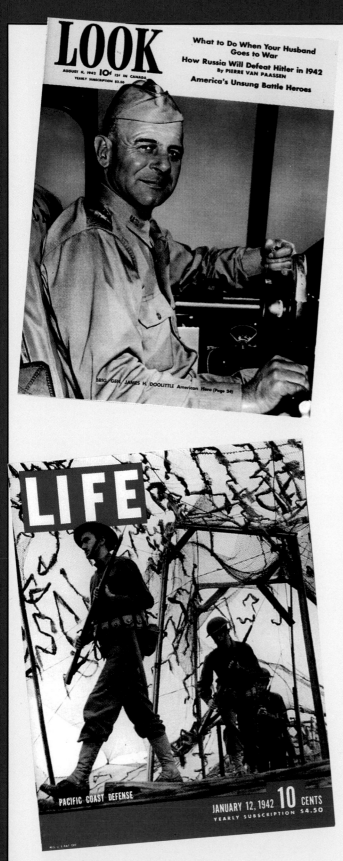

General James Doolittle was an instant hero after his April 1942 Tokyo raid. He went on to command air forces in Europe and Asia.

Life and *Time* were the two main news/photo magazines of the war years.

Magazines provided a large, ready market for cover propaganda art to further the war effort.

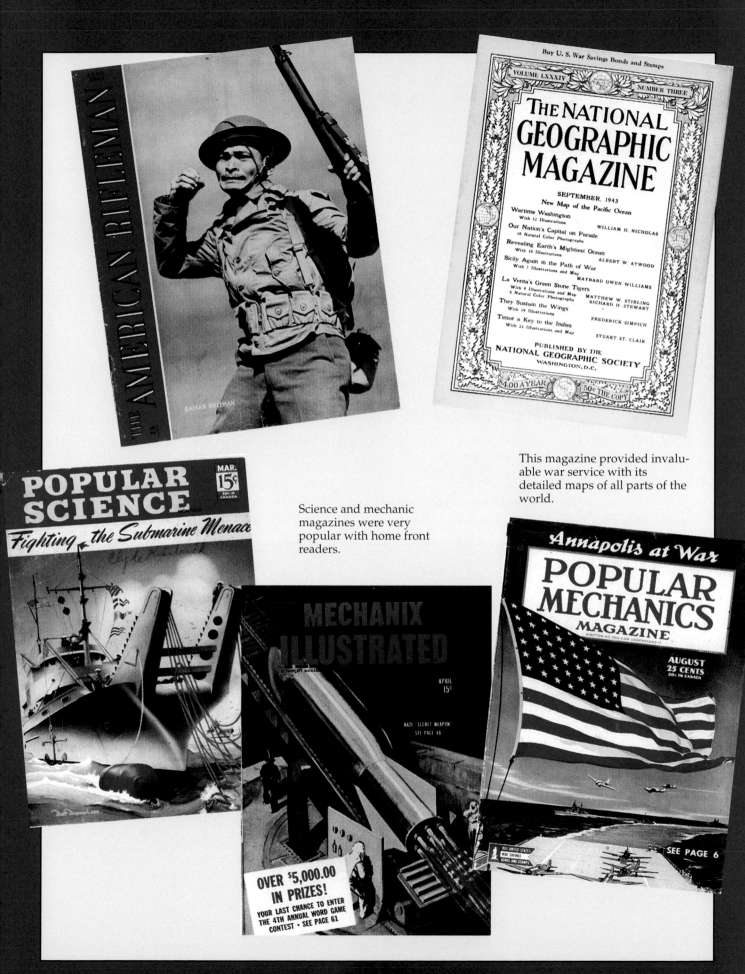

This magazine provided invaluable war service with its detailed maps of all parts of the world.

Science and mechanic magazines were very popular with home front readers.

War Maps of the World

Lowell Thomas was a popular radio announcer whose adventures spanned many decades of the century.

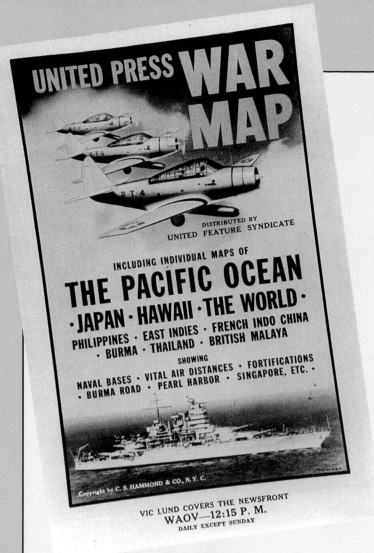

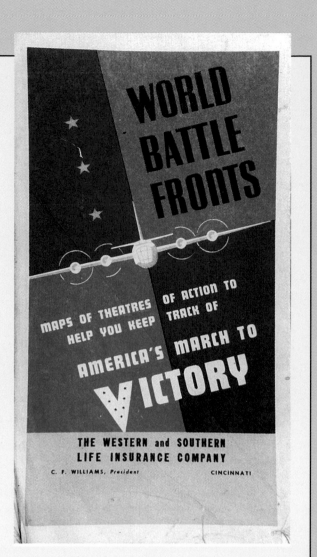

This Greyhound map showed the extent of military facilities throughout the United States.

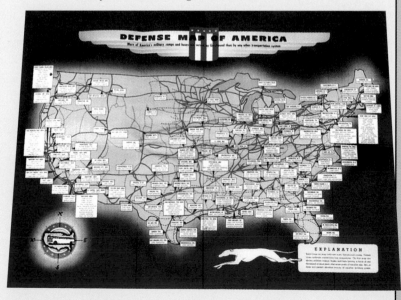

Menu Planning in Wartime

MEAL PLANNING under rationing will need all the intelligent consideration with which the housekeeper is endowed. It demands an understanding of nutrition principles, a facility in combining foods for a meal, the best methods of cookery, and more than a dash of ingenuity to make meals appetizing and acceptable. It also calls for cooperation on the part of the man of the family and the children. No complaints about casserole dishes and no "expressed at the table" wails for absent steak or roast beef!

Family problems vary with the number in the group, the age of the children and with outside activities. It is possible to make a more varied selection of meat when there are four or more ration books to be used, than when there are fewer. If there are little children, extra points may need to be spent for them. Although they do not eat such large portions as do older persons, it may be necessary to make special provision for a meat for them when the family is to have a combination casserole dish. If some of the family eat lunch away from home, there will be more leeway in planning dinner.

A tentative plan should be made for the whole week, having in mind the amount of table and cooking fat which must be purchased or which is on hand for use in cooking. The points which you are able to use on meat and cheese will depend largely on this. When possible, it will be well to save some of a week's points for use later in the month, as this will allow the eventual purchase of a larger roast. The use of fish, chicken, dried beans, peas, and lentils for a number of meals will be point saving. The latter require blue stamps, but the point value is low. The expenditure of the remaining blue stamps will vary with the supply of fresh vegetables and fruit in the market.

There is more to menu planning, however, than deciding how to use points to good advantage. The food used for the three meals should contribute the necessary minerals and vitamins as well as the proteins. The daily menu must be adequate in all respects so that we may be well-fed from the nutrition standpoint. The Nutrition and Food Conservation Branch of the Food Distribution Administration, United States Department of Agriculture, has recently furnished us with a revised nutrition yardstick, which should be used when the weekly menus are planned and for checking after revision to fit market conditions.

FARMERS!
Uncle Sam asks you...
to get ready for the census taker

In January the U.S. Census Bureau will ask you about 1944 crops–amount–value–acres–livestock–tractors–labor hired and tenure

THE LAW REQUIRING YOUR REPORTS MAKES THEM CONFIDENTIAL

SHOOT TO KILL!

PROTECT YOUR VICTORY GARDEN

Menu for Family of Two

SUNDAY

BREAKFAST
Orange sections
Griddle cakes   Syrup   Coffee

DINNER
Vegetable appetizer
Oven-cooked broilers
Creamed new potatoes   Peas
Raspberry Ice

SUPPER
Salad bowl
Cottage cheese
French bread
Cup cakes   Tea

MONDAY

BREAKFAST
Stewed prunes
Ready-to-eat cereal
Toast   Marmalade   Coffee

LUNCHEON
Potato and pea soup
Mixed vegetable salad
Cake   Tea

DINNER
Creamed eggs on toast
(bacon garnish)
Spinach
Jellied fruit

TUESDAY

BREAKFAST
Orange juice
Cooked cereal
Bran muffins   Coffee

LUNCHEON
Peanut butter sandwiches
Raw carrot salad
Tea cookies

DINNER
Swedish meat balls
Potatoes with parsley
Buttered beets
Baked custard

WEDNESDAY

BREAKFAST
Grapefruit
Ready-to-eat cereal
Boiled eggs
Hot rolls   Coffee

LUNCHEON
Beet soup
Watercress salad
Cookies   Tea

DINNER
Spaghetti with meat balls
Mixed green salad
Baked custard with strawberries

THURSDAY

BREAKFAST
Stewed prunes
Cooked cereal
Toasted rolls   Jam   Coffee

LUNCHEON
Bacon sandwiches
Watercress salad
Stewed rhubarb   Tea

DINNER
Cheese soufflé
Baked potatoes   Carrots
Strawberry cream

FRIDAY

BREAKFAST
Grapefruit juice
Ready-to-eat cereal
Poached eggs on toast
Coffee

LUNCHEON
Avocado salad
Watercress sandwiches
Cookies   Tea

DINNER
Poached fish   Pickle sauce
Mashed potatoes
String beans
Rhubarb tarts

SATURDAY

BREAKFAST
Orange juice
Cooked cereal
Coffee cake   Coffee

LUNCHEON
Fish chowder
Vegetable salad
Marmalade toast   Tea

DINNER
Veal cube steaks   Brown gravy
Boiled rice   Greens
Lemon jelly

The Sun
NEW YORK

WAR TIME
Cook Book

**MENUS, RECIPES AND CANNING INFORMATION
TO HELP MAKE YOUR RATION POINTS GO FURTHER**

By
EDITH·M·BARBER
FAMED FOOD EDITOR OF THE NEW YORK SUN

25¢

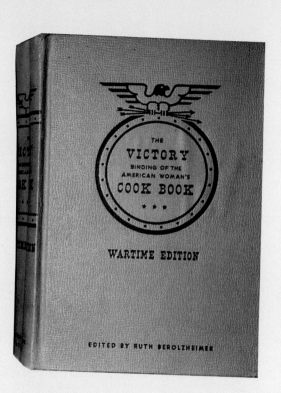

THE
VICTORY
BINDING OF THE
AMERICAN WOMAN'S
COOK BOOK
★ ★ ★

WARTIME EDITION

EDITED BY RUTH BEROLZHEIMER

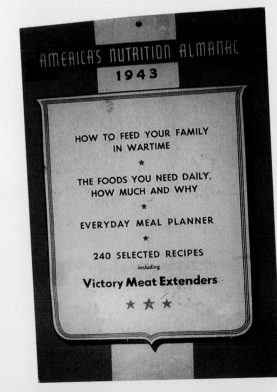

AMERICA'S NUTRITION ALMANAC
1943

HOW TO FEED YOUR FAMILY
IN WARTIME

★

THE FOODS YOU NEED DAILY,
HOW MUCH AND WHY

★

EVERYDAY MEAL PLANNER

★

240 SELECTED RECIPES
including
Victory Meat Extenders

★ ★ ★

VICTORY COOK BOOK
How to
**EAT WELL · · · LIVE WELL · · ·
PLAN BALANCED MEALS · · ·**
under
FOOD RATIONING

Photo courtesy McCall's Magazine

Simple recipes that save ration points, show you how to feed your
family well without scarce and expensive foods. Every housewife's
job is to maintain her family's health and spirits. This book is published to promote Healthy Eating and Healthy Living in every home.

FREE with purchase of LYSOL

CRISCO'S Victory
WHITE CAKE

½ cup Crisco
¾ cup sugar
½ teaspoon salt
1 teaspoon vanilla
½ cup corn syrup

2 cups sifted cake flour
2 teaspoons baking powder
¾ cup milk
3 egg whites

Blend Crisco, sugar, salt and vanilla. Add corn syrup. Sift flour and baking powder and add alternately with milk to Crisco mixture. Fold in egg whites beaten stiff but not dry. Bake in two round 8-inch "Criscoed" layer pans in a moderate oven (360° F.) for 35 minutes, or (for a one-layer cake) in a 9-inch square "Criscoed" pan for 40 minutes.

Cool cake. If a 2-layer cake, frost with Chocolate or Lady Baltimore Icing, below. If a single layer, cover top and sides with the Chocolate Icing.

CHOCOLATE ICING
(Use with 2-layer or single layer White Cake, or with Victory [Yellow] Layer Cake)

2 squares unsweetened chocolate
1⅓ cups (14 or 15 oz. can) sweetened condensed milk
1 teaspoon vanilla

Melt chocolate in top of double boiler. Add milk and stir over rapidly boiling water 5-10 minutes, or until thick. Add vanilla and beat to a spreading consistency. (For a CHOCOLATE PEPPERMINT flavor, omit the vanilla, substituting one tablespoon water and a few drops of peppermint flavoring.)

For a 2-layer cake, spread between layers and on top and sides. If peppermint flavor is used, you can decorate top with small soft white peppermint candies.

LADY BALTIMORE ICING AND FILLING
(Use with 2-layer White Cake)

Honey Icing

½ cup honey   1 egg white   ⅛ teaspoon salt

Heat honey over hot water. Beat egg white with salt until stiff. Pour hot honey slowly over egg white, beating constantly. Continue beating until thick and fluffy.

Filling

½ cup raisins
¼ cup figs

¼ cup nutmeats
¼ cup maraschino cherries

Chop all ingredients together until fine. Blend with ¼ cup icing. Spread between layers.

Cover top and sides of cake with icing. Decorate top with walnuts and cherries.

CRISCO'S Victory
YELLOW CAKE

½ cup Crisco
½ cup sugar
½ teaspoon salt
1 teaspoon vanilla
2 eggs

½ cup corn syrup
1¾ cups flour
2½ teaspoons baking powder
¾ cup milk

Blend together Crisco, sugar, salt, vanilla and eggs. Add corn syrup. Sift dry ingredients together and add alternately with milk to the first mixture. Bake in two 8-inch "Criscoed" layer pans in a moderately hot oven (375° F.) 30-35 minutes.

Cool cake. Put layers together with Apricot Surprise Filling, or frost cake with Chocolate or Honey Mallow Icing, below.

APRICOT SURPRISE FILLING
(Use with Victory Layer Cake)

2 cups dried apricots
⅓ cup sugar
1 tablespoon lemon juice

Soak apricots for several hours in enough water to cover. Cook apricots with sugar until thick and smooth. Cool. Add lemon juice. Spread between layers.

To decorate top of cake, place a lacy paper doily (wrong side up) on top of cake. Sift on confectioners sugar till doily is completely covered. Lift up carefully and you will have a lacy design.

HONEY MALLOW ICING
(Use with Victory Layer Cake)

½ cup honey
½ cup white corn syrup
⅛ teaspoon salt
1 egg white

Mix warm honey and corn syrup together. Beat egg white with salt until stiff. Pour warm syrup over beaten egg slowly, beating until thick enough to spread. Use between layers and on top and sides of cake.

Note: 1 cup corn syrup may be used—omitting the honey—in which case, add 1½ teaspoons vanilla.

IT IS A VITALLY URGENT JOB!

Before the war, many of the fats and oils from which glycerine is made—almost two billion pounds of them—were imported from the Far East; from the Philippines and the Jap-held islands of the Pacific.

That important source has been cut off. At the same time the military needs of this country and of our Allies have tremendously increased the need for glycerine.

But *enough fats and greases are thrown away* or poured down sink drains every year *to equal the total of fats and oils we formerly imported from the Far East!*

If every housewife in America would save and turn in only one pound of used cooking fats and greases every month, it would produce enough glycerine to make over half a billion pounds of smokeless powder.

A pound a month is only a tablespoonful a day. A tablespoonful a day—to help shorten the war and save the lives of thousands of boys who are fighting so that we may survive. Just a tablespoonful a day—it isn't much to ask for, is it?

YOU CAN DO IT— EVEN WITH RATIONING

With the rationing of meats and cooking fats and oils, you naturally have less fats. You're using them carefully. Using them over and over again.

But the Government doesn't want your fats—even to make gunpowder—until you've gotten all the food use out of them.

When you have finished with them—when they are too dark or too strong flavored to cook with—then save them for gunpowder. Pan drippings, soup skimmings, old shortening, *any* kind of used fats—*save* them—and turn them in promptly to your meat dealer.

Even with rationing, the average family of four persons can buy, on the point system, four-hundred-and-sixteen pounds of meat a year and another one-hundred-and-thirty pounds of butter and shortening. Out of all this, the Government is asking for only twelve pounds of recovered fat, a year.

A tablespoonful a day—that's the least you can contribute to Victory. And if you can *save more* than a tablespoonful of fat—this country needs every drop—desperately.

LET'S SAVE...AND SAVE LIVES!

TO AMERICAN HOMEMAKERS

March 26, 1943

You have many and heavy responsibilities on the home front of the war we are fighting. Your management of the civilian food supply is vital to winning the war. Every scrap of food value must be conserved. The need for American food is becoming even greater than the huge supply we are producing. I urge that you make sure that all the food value is obtained from the fats that come into your kitchen. Our superiority in fats and oils over the Axis nations is one of our great sources of food strength in this war. Your help in getting the maximum food value out of all fats and oils coming into your household will aid in maintaining our superior food position.

But, fats fight in two ways. They are a source of military supplies as well as of food values. Fats are the source of glycerine to make gunpowder, explosives, medical supplies needed by the fighting men. Therefore, your job in the kitchen is not only to get full food value from fats, but to salvage every ounce after you have made maximum use of it for food. In peacetime hundreds of millions of pounds of fats went to waste in our kitchens. We cannot afford to continue this in wartime. I ask that you save fats that have served their food usefulness and turn them in to your Government to make munitions.

This booklet tells how and why. I know we can count on your help.

Claude R. Wickard

Claude R. Wickard
Secretary of Agriculture

YOU CAN HELP SHORTEN THIS WAR!

WE must win this war. We must win if it takes every man we have and every dollar, too. But that won't be necessary if we all realize what it takes to win, and what each of us must do.

Every day of war costs thousands of lives and millions of dollars. If the war can be shortened even by one day, the saving in lives alone should be worth any sacrifice we can make.

YOU can help shorten this war—and save American lives—*right in your kitchen!*

HOW? By saving at least a tablespoon of used cooking fats *and greases every day.*

WHY? Because used cooking fats contain glycerine and glycerine is needed for gunpowder. We are short of glycerine—short millions of pounds of it. One important source which has not yet been tapped to the limit remains. That source is the used fats from the kitchens of America.

SAVING WASTE FATS IS YOUR JOB AND—

SAVE AT LEAST ONE TABLESPOON OF THESE FATS EVERY DAY!

SAVE
the drippings left in your broil pan after cooking meats, fish, poultry, etc.

SAVE
the grease that rises to the top of stews and meat-base and poultry soups.

SAVE
the grease left over from frying bacon, pork, poultry, sausage, etc.

SAVE
the greases in your baking pan after baking and roasting meats and poultry.

SAVE
solid fats cut from meats in preparation, or left over at the table. Solid fats should be melted down when the oven is on and strained into a container.

SAVE
used lard, vegetable shortenings and cooking oils after all the food values have been secured.

AND YOU SAVE LIVES!

No Eggs!

No Sugar! No Shortening!

EGGLESS CHOCOLATE CAKE   HONEY SPICE CAKE

JELLY ROLL
(recipe page 6)

Wartime Recipes for Cakes and Frostings

They won't believe you, but it's true. No eggs at all and only ½ cup shortening in this tender, delicate, quick chocolate cake that took you only 1 minute to beat. The secret in two words—Swans Down.

The sugar jar's never even open when you make this cake. For it's sweetened with honey and raisins, topped with nuts, and needs no frosting. Yet like all Swans Down cakes, it's beautifully moist, fine.

EGGLESS CHOCOLATE CAKE

2 squares Baker's Un-sweetened Chocolate	¾ teaspoon soda
1 cup milk	¾ teaspoon salt
1¾ cups sifted Swans Down Cake Flour	1 cup sugar
	½ cup shortening
	1 teaspoon vanilla

Combine chocolate and milk in top of double boiler and cook over rapidly boiling water 5 minutes, stirring occasionally. Blend with rotary egg beater; cool.

Sift flour once, measure, add soda, salt, and sugar, and sift together three times. Cream shortening; add flour, vanilla, and chocolate mixture and stir until all flour is dampened. Then beat vigorously 1 minute. Bake in two greased and lightly floured 8-inch layer pans in moderate oven (375° F.) 20 minutes, or until done. Spread Quick Orange Frosting (page 6), or Cocoa Minute Frosting (page 8), or Easy Fluffy Frosting (page 7) between layers and on top of cake.

Cocoa Cake. Substitute ¼ cup Baker's Breakfast Cocoa for chocolate. Sift it with dry ingredients; add cold milk with vanilla.

4

HONEY SPICE CAKE
(2 eggs)

2 cups sifted Swans Down Cake Flour	2 egg yolks, unbeaten
2 teaspoons Calumet Baking Powder	½ cup milk
¾ teaspoon salt	¾ cup chopped raisins
1½ teaspoons allspice	1 teaspoon vanilla
½ cup shortening	2 egg whites
1 teaspoon grated lemon rind	½ cup chopped walnut meats
¾ cup honey	

Sift flour once, measure, add baking powder, salt, and allspice, and sift together three times. Cream shortening with lemon rind; add honey gradually, beating well after each addition. Add ¼ of flour and beat until smooth and well blended. Add egg yolks, one at a time, beating well after each. Add remaining flour in thirds, alternately with milk in halves, beating very well after each addition. Add raisins with last addition of flour. Add vanilla. Beat egg whites until stiff enough to hold up in moist peaks. Stir quickly but thoroughly into batter. Turn into greased 8x8x2-inch pan and sprinkle with nut meats. Bake in moderate oven (350° F.) 55 minutes, or until done.

5

MEAT RECIPE BOOK

VICTORY MEAT EXTENDERS

Compliments **NATIONAL LIVE STOCK AND MEAT BOARD**

Suggestion: Close cover and run a string through hole — then hang booklet in convenient place for handy reference. ↗

CONTENTS

Foreword

Because our fighting men must be properly fed, the supply of many foods is limited here at home. All of us are willing to make this sacrifice, because we know that the food we do without will help speed final victory.

However, wartime rationing and the disappearance of familiar items from grocers' shelves have created many unique food-keeping problems. Every refrigerator user faces them today.

Shopping is done less frequently. Food for the weekend is purchased as early as Wednesday. People are buying "variety" meats they never used before. Preparing foods they used to buy in cans. Making greater use of leftovers.

Until Victory is won, our resources are pledged to the manufacture of more and better weapons for our armed forces. At the same time, we want to do everything possible to help refrigerator users solve their new food-keeping problems. We especially want to help the users of the more than **7** million Frigidaires we have built and sold.

That is why we prepared WARTIME SUGGESTIONS. It is based on our years of experience as a food-keeping authority, and represents the combined thinking of our home economists, engineers, and service experts. We hope the suggestions it contains will help you during this critical period.

Frigidaire Products of Canada, Ltd. Toronto, Ont.

Frigidaire Division General Motors Corporation Dayton, Ohio

How cheese helps with your main dish problem

IN THESE DAYS of rationed foods, American homemakers are finding many ways to serve appetizing, balanced meals at a very low cost in ration points. For instance, an entire meal can be planned around a splendid cheese main dish.

Cheese is an economical, protein food . . . and it is *all* food . . . there is *no* waste. With as little as one-half pound of cheese, in combination with other more plentiful foods, you can prepare a delicious main dish that will serve 4 to 8 persons.

The recipes in this book have been especially prepared to *extend* the cheese you buy—make a little go a long way! In each recipe we have kept in mind your wartime marketing problems and your budget of time, ration points and money.

While good cheese adds fine flavor, these recipes use it to *complete* the protein of other more plentiful foods. (Beans, for instance, supply protein but *not* the high-quality protein of cheese or meat.)

These dishes are nutritionally sound solutions for your main-dish problem. We think you'll find them to be thoroughly practical . . . and praised by your family, just because *they taste so good.*

Marye Dahnke

DIRECTOR, KRAFT HOME ECONOMICS KITCHEN

Buy YOUR share in the NEW VINCENNES NOW!

Your EXTRA WAR BOND says... They can't sink an INDIANA FIGHTING SHIP

Record of Ownership of US ★ SAVINGS BONDS

This box was built by a man who carried around a monkey to war bond drives. It is presumed that both monkey and man promoted the purchase of the bonds.

Rationing and Scrap

DON'T FORGET!
SUGAR STAMP #13
Good for 5 pounds
JUNE 1 thru AUG. 15
C and CH PURE CANE SUGAR
EVERY KIND FOR EVERY USE

TOKIO KID SAY
BOOM PLANES
SAVED FROM
BOX OF SCRAP
MAKE SO VERY
UNHAPPY JAP

RATION STAMPS

When you Bake — Bake with Maca

For Gunpowder
SAVE WASTE FATS
Rush Them to Your Meat Dealer

VICTORY SERVICE LEAGUE
MEMBER
VS
SERVICE for VICTORY
SAVE THE WHEELS
THAT SERVE AMERICA

Transportation

They've got more important places to go than you!...

Save Rubber
CHECK YOUR TIRES NOW

I'll carry mine too!

TRUCKS AND TIRES MUST LAST TILL VICTORY

The Order of Railroad Telegraphers

O H COATS   V   2110-54

JUNE 30, 1945

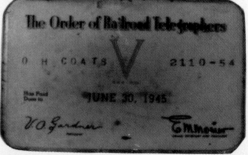

Worth REMEMBERING

Throughout the war, railroads provided 97% of the transportation for military personnel traveling on duty, and carried over 90% of all the military freight.

Association of *American Railroads*

American railroads were an essential part of the nation's transportation network. They transported raw materials, finished goods and troops to east and west coast ports.

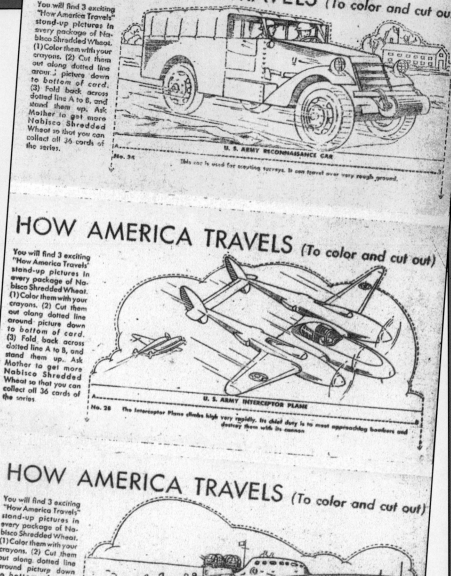

HOW AMERICA TRAVELS (To color and cut out)

You will find 3 exciting "How America Travels" stand-up pictures in every package of Nabisco Shredded Wheat. (1) Color them with your crayons. (2) Cut them out along dotted line around picture down to bottom of card. (3) Fold back across dotted line A to B, and stand them up. Ask Mother to get more Nabisco Shredded Wheat so that you can collect all 36 cards of the series.

U. S. ARMY RECONNAISANCE CAR

No. 34   This car is used for scouting surveys. It can travel over very rough ground.

HOW AMERICA TRAVELS (To color and cut out)

You will find 3 exciting "How America Travels" stand-up pictures in every package of Nabisco Shredded Wheat. (1) Color them with your crayons. (2) Cut them out along dotted line around picture down to bottom of card. (3) Fold back across dotted line A to B, and stand them up. Ask Mother to get more Nabisco Shredded Wheat so that you can collect all 36 cards of the series.

U. S. ARMY INTERCEPTOR PLANE

No. 28   The Interceptor Plane climbs high very rapidly. Its chief duty is to meet approaching bombers and destroy them with its cannon

HOW AMERICA TRAVELS (To color and cut out)

You will find 3 exciting "How America Travels" stand-up pictures in every package of Nabisco Shredded Wheat. (1) Color them with your crayons. (2) Cut them out along dotted line around picture down to bottom of card. (3) Fold back across dotted line A to B, and stand them up. Ask Mother to get more Nabisco Shredded Wheat so that you can collect all 36 cards of the series.

U. S. NAVY "MOSQUITO BOAT"

No. 23   The Mosquito boats are very fast. Run by three motors, they carry torpedoes and do hit-and-run duty.

Although recognized as a necessary evil, gas rationing was not popular with the American public. In the east it went into effect in May 1942, the rest of the country was saved until after the Presidential elections in November 1942. A thirty-five mph speed limit also was instituted.

These cards, slightly reduced, were found in every Nabisco Shredded Wheat box.

PLANES, TANKS, GUNS and BREAD

Bread, too, is a vital element in national defense. And its mass production—like that of planes, tanks, and guns—depends on adequate and efficient railroad transportation.

In addition to moving the huge 1941 wheat crop, the railroads this year were called on to move — from crowded grain-belt elevators to distant storage points—millions of bushels of grain left over from last year's harvest.

They answered that call by providing freight cars for every bushel of grain which could be unloaded at any market, or for which storage space could be found anywhere.

More than that, while the wheat movement was in progress, the railroads continued to supply—adequately and smoothly — all the railroad service needed for a mounting production of planes, tanks, guns, and all the other implements of national defense.

NO. 60

Association of AMERICAN RAILROADS Washington, D. C.

The Arsenal of Democracy

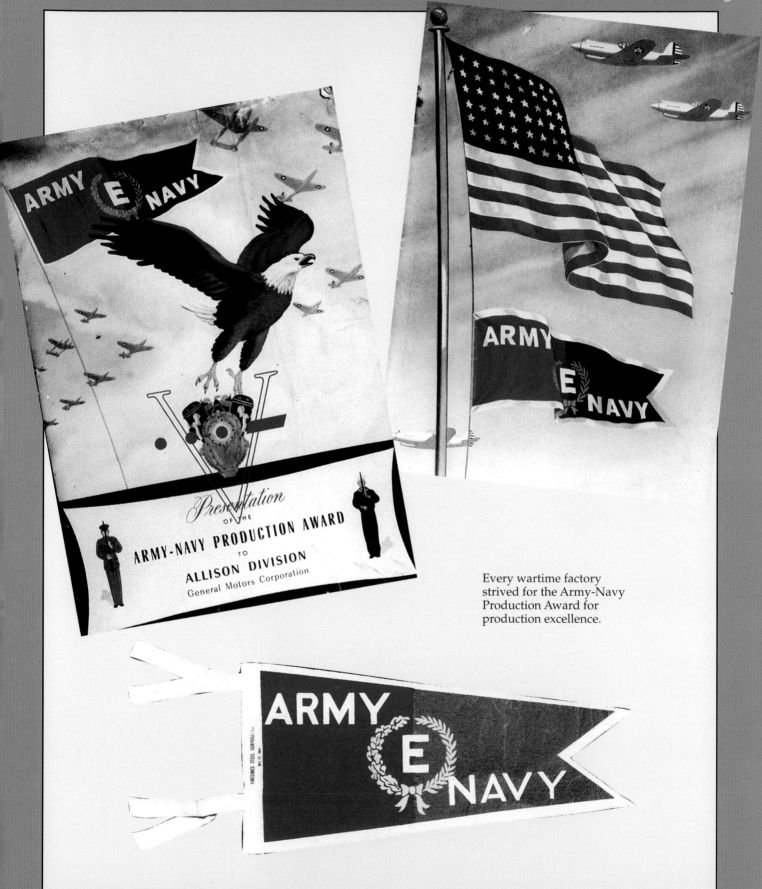

Presentation OF THE ARMY-NAVY PRODUCTION AWARD TO ALLISON DIVISION General Motors Corporation

Every wartime factory strived for the Army-Navy Production Award for production excellence.

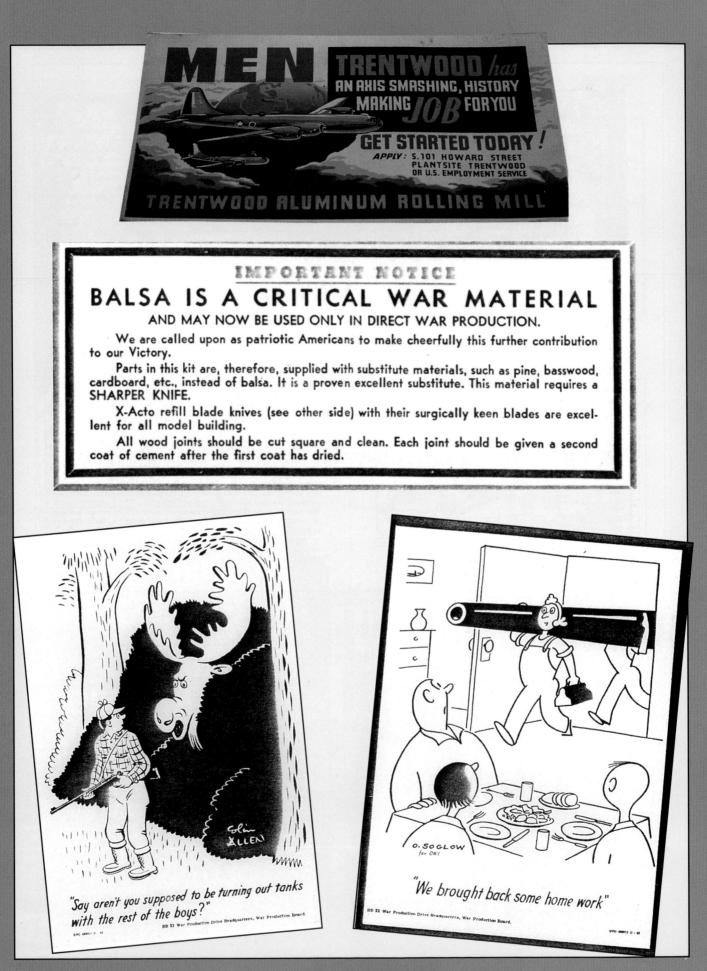

MEN TRENTWOOD *has* AN AXIS SMASHING, HISTORY MAKING **JOB** FOR YOU

GET STARTED TODAY!
APPLY: S.101 HOWARD STREET
PLANTSITE TRENTWOOD
OR U.S. EMPLOYMENT SERVICE

TRENTWOOD ALUMINUM ROLLING MILL

IMPORTANT NOTICE

BALSA IS A CRITICAL WAR MATERIAL

AND MAY NOW BE USED ONLY IN DIRECT WAR PRODUCTION.

We are called upon as patriotic Americans to make cheerfully this further contribution to our Victory.

Parts in this kit are, therefore, supplied with substitute materials, such as pine, basswood, cardboard, etc., instead of balsa. It is a proven excellent substitute. This material requires a SHARPER KNIFE.

X-Acto refill blade knives (see other side) with their surgically keen blades are excellent for all model building.

All wood joints should be cut square and clean. Each joint should be given a second coat of cement after the first coat has dried.

"Say aren't you supposed to be turning out tanks with the rest of the boys?"

BD 23 War Production Drive Headquarters, War Production Board.

"We brought back some home work"

BD 22 War Production Drive Headquarters, War Production Board.

USO

These small sound sheets gave the serviceman a small touch of home. You could call this the world's first "voice mail."

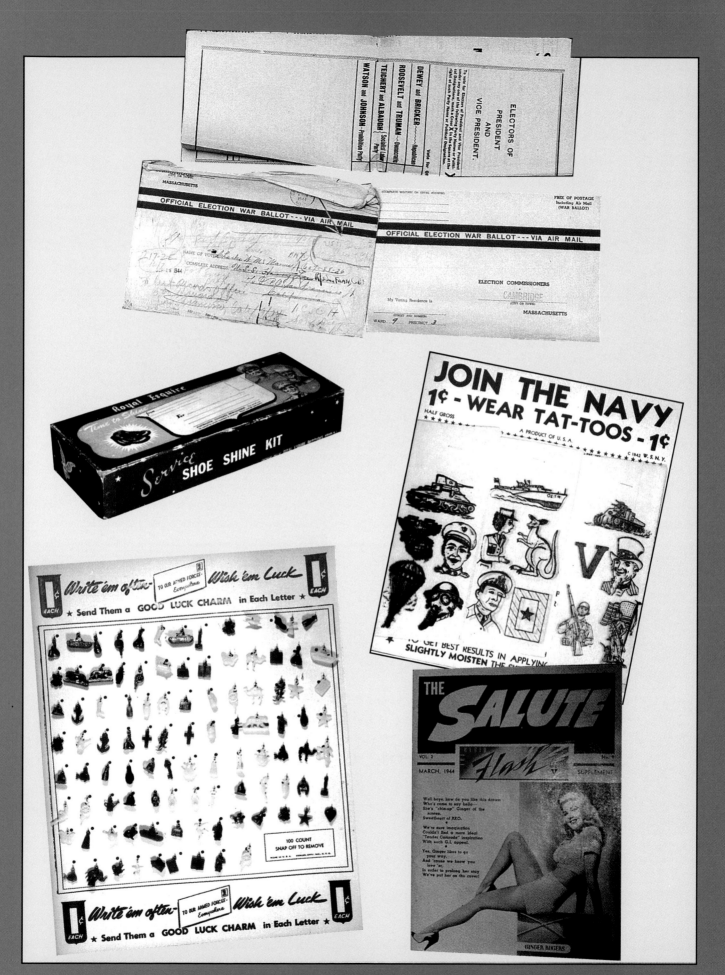

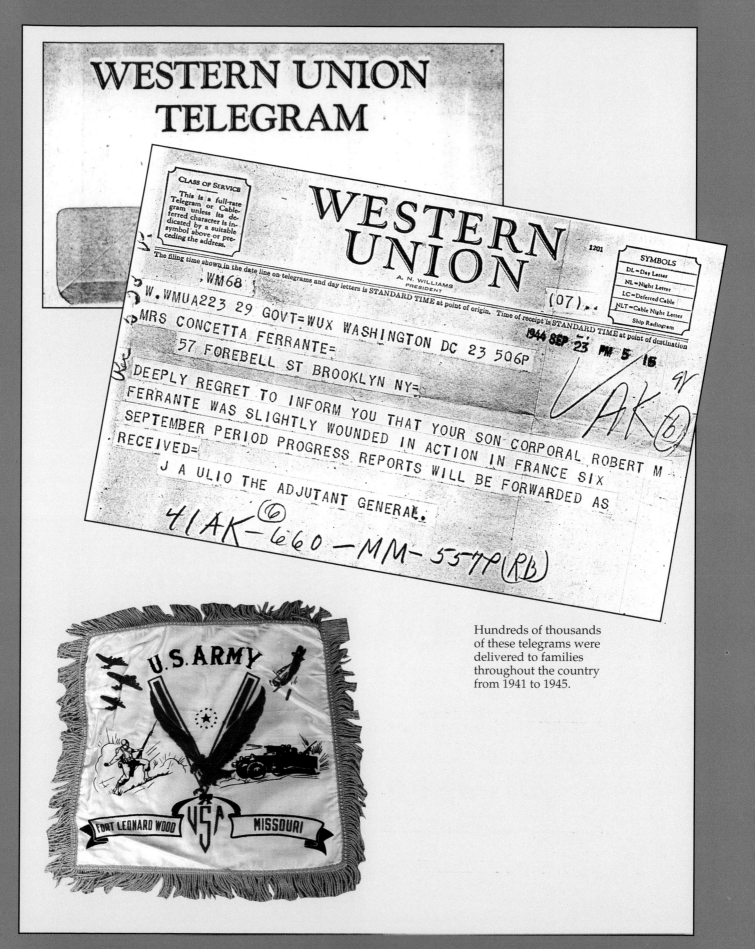

WESTERN UNION TELEGRAM

WESTERN UNION

A. N. WILLIAMS
PRESIDENT

CLASS OF SERVICE

This is a full-rate Telegram or Cablegram unless its deferred character is indicated by a suitable symbol above or preceding the address.

The filing time shown in the date line on telegrams and day letters is STANDARD TIME at point of origin. Time of receipt is STANDARD TIME at point of destination

1201

(07)

SYMBOLS

DL = Day Letter
NL = Night Letter
LC = Deferred Cable
NLT = Cable Night Letter
Ship Radiogram

WM68

W.WMUA223 29 GOVT=WUX WASHINGTON DC 23 506P

1944 SEP 23 PM 5 16

MRS CONCETTA FERRANTE=

57 FOREBELL ST BROOKLYN NY=

DEEPLY REGRET TO INFORM YOU THAT YOUR SON CORPORAL ROBERT M
FERRANTE WAS SLIGHTLY WOUNDED IN ACTION IN FRANCE SIX
SEPTEMBER PERIOD PROGRESS REPORTS WILL BE FORWARDED AS
RECEIVED=

J A ULIO THE ADJUTANT GENERAL.

41AK-660-MM-557P(RB)

U.S. ARMY

FORT LEONARD WOOD — USA — MISSOURI

Hundreds of thousands
of these telegrams were
delivered to families
throughout the country
from 1941 to 1945.

Correspondence

TE/.35¢

UNITED STATES ARMY

U.S. SERVICE STATIONERY

Greeting Cards

MERRY XMAS

1944

MERRY XMAS 1944

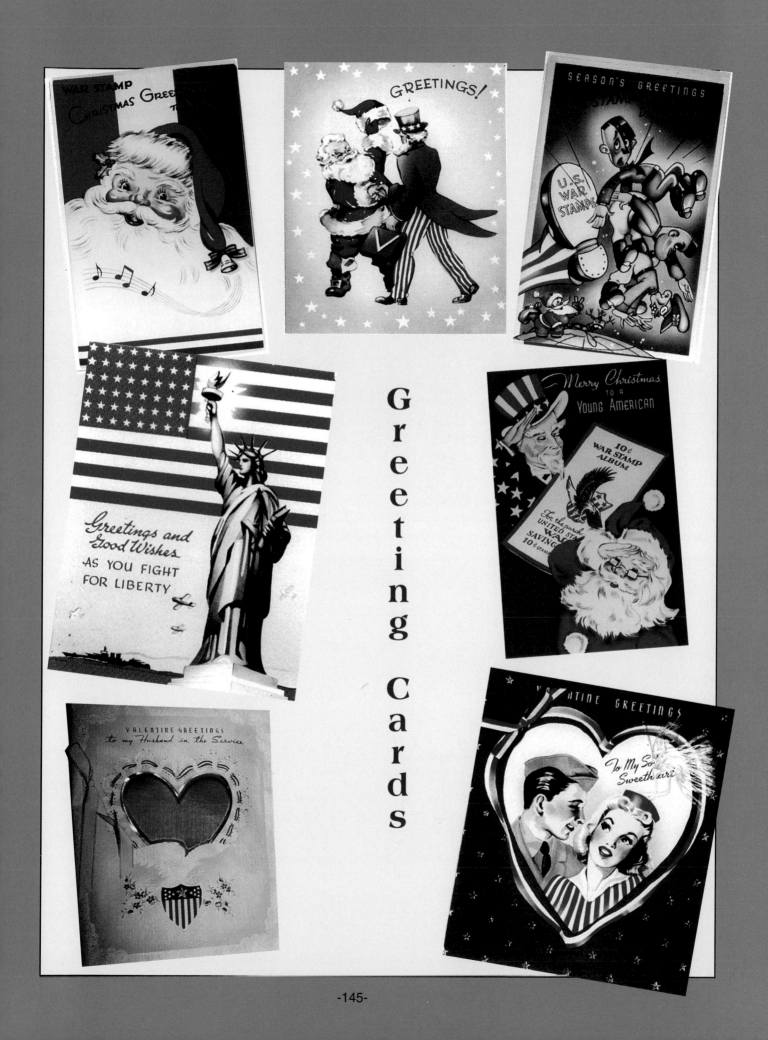

Greeting Cards

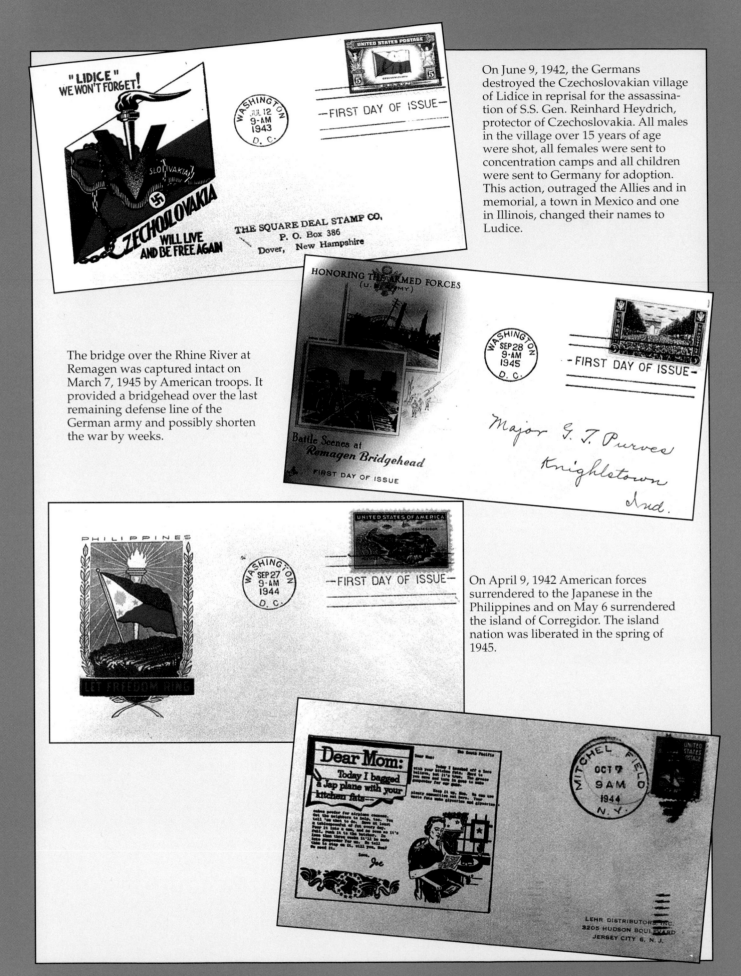

On June 9, 1942, the Germans destroyed the Czechoslovakian village of Lidice in reprisal for the assassination of S.S. Gen. Reinhard Heydrich, protector of Czechoslovakia. All males in the village over 15 years of age were shot, all females were sent to concentration camps and all children were sent to Germany for adoption. This action, outraged the Allies and in memorial, a town in Mexico and one in Illinois, changed their names to Ludice.

The bridge over the Rhine River at Remagen was captured intact on March 7, 1945 by American troops. It provided a bridgehead over the last remaining defense line of the German army and possibly shorten the war by weeks.

On April 9, 1942 American forces surrendered to the Japanese in the Philippines and on May 6 surrendered the island of Corregidor. The island nation was liberated in the spring of 1945.

THIS IS THE ENEMY

WORK FOR VICTORY

WAKE

with the FIGHTING SPIRIT of the

WAKE ISLAND MARINES

Mrs. O. W. Wilson
Box 133
Bakersville
North Carolina

VJ

WE HAVE AVENGED
PEARL HARBOR

Miss Betty W. Harmay
310 Quail St
Albany 3,
N.Y.

FIGHT FOR VICTORY

Lt. J.H. Van Alsburg USNR
2222 Eye St. N.W
Washington
D.C.

Kiska Island in Alaska's Aleutian Chain was occupied by Japanese forces in June 1942. They evacuated the island undetected in late July 1943 not August 21, 1943.

Children and The War

This watercolor box was made out of cardboard as opposed to tin which was used before and after the war.

Johnson Smith and Co. was a large mail order house that sold thousands of different novelty items to children throughout the country.

Boys! Build your own scale model of the AIRCRAFT CARRIER and B-25 Bombers that raided Tokio! THIS SET contains carrier and 10 Bombers with COMPLETE INSTRUCTIONS for assembling. Read the Story of THE TOKIO RAIDERS on back of this package

The famous Doolittle Tokyo raid of April 18, 1942 spawned this children's game. There were 16 B-25s and 80 crewmen who flew off the USS *Hornet* and made the first bombing raid over Japan.

The graphics on the boxes of wartime games were very dramatic and are prime collector items today when they can be found.

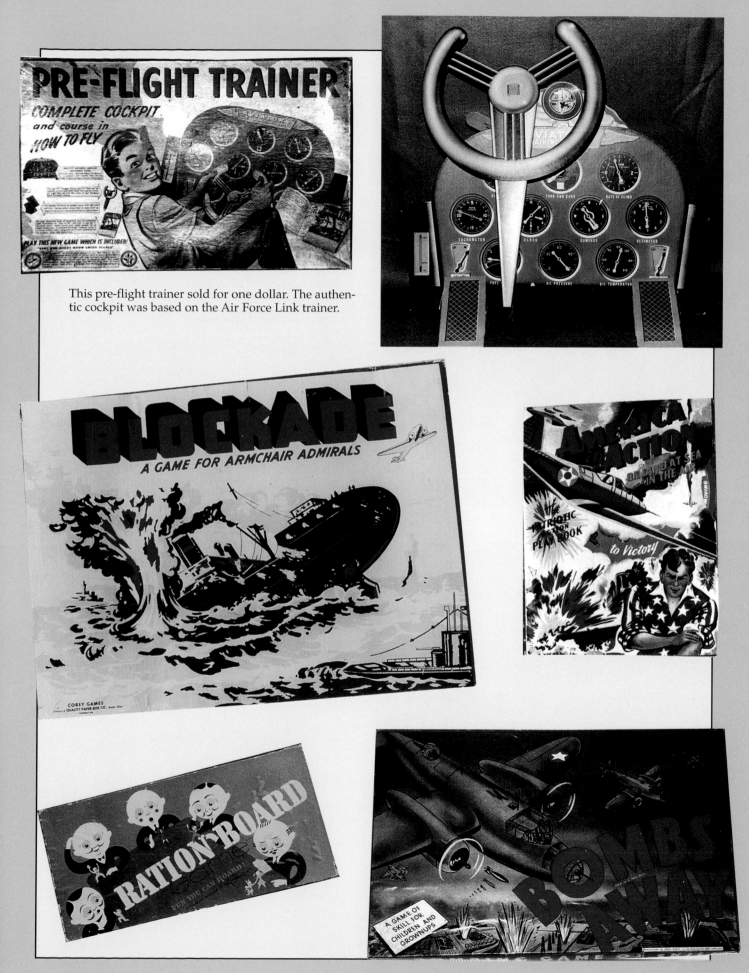

This pre-flight trainer sold for one dollar. The authentic cockpit was based on the Air Force Link trainer.

A dart board with a Japanese character in the middle.

A "Capture Hitler" marble game produced by Harry W. Standidge Company in 1942.

Wheaties 1944 series of "Tru-Flite Fighter Models" is probably the most famous and common wartime premium. These terrific cardboard copies flew a long way if a penny was glued inside the nose for balance.

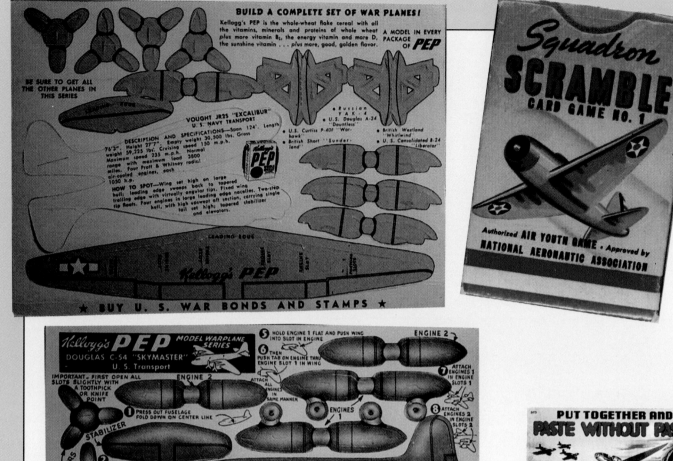

BUILD A COMPLETE SET OF WAR PLANES!

Kellogg's PEP is the whole-wheat flake cereal with all the vitamins, minerals and proteins of whole wheat plus more vitamin B₁, the energy vitamin and more D, the sunshine vitamin . . . plus more, good, golden flavor.

A MODEL IN EVERY PACKAGE OF PEP

BE SURE TO GET ALL THE OTHER PLANES IN THIS SERIES

VOUGHT JR2S "EXCALIBUR" U. S. NAVY TRANSPORT

DESCRIPTION AND SPECIFICATIONS—Span 124', Length 76'3". Height 27'7". Empty weight 30,500 lbs. Gross weight 59,225 lbs. Cruising speed 150 m.p.h. Maximum speed 235 m.p.h. Normal range with maximum load 3800 miles. Four Pratt & Whitney radial air-cooled engines, each 1050 h.p.

HOW TO SPOT—Wing set high on large hull, leading edge sweeps back to tapered trailing edge with virtually angular tips. Fixed wing tip floats. Four engines in large leading edge nacelles. Two-step hull, with high upswept aft section, carrying single tail set high, tapered stabilizer and elevators.

• Russian YAK-4
• U.S. Douglas A-24 "Dauntless"
• U.S. Curtiss P-40F "War-hawk"
• British Short "Sunderland"
• British Westland "Whirlwind"
• U. S. Consolidated B-24 "Liberator"

LEADING EDGE

Kellogg's PEP

★ BUY U. S. WAR BONDS AND STAMPS ★

THIS IS AN AUTHENTIC SCALE MODEL SUITABLE FOR SILHOUETTE IDENTIFICATION • NOT A FLYING MODEL •

VICTORY
IF YOU SOLVE THIS PORTION OF THE ALLIES'

MAJOR WAR PROBLEM
IT IS TOUGH BUT CAN BE DONE

A PATRIOTIC, INTERESTING PUZZLE
THE PROBLEM IS TO JOIN ALL 10 NATIONS TOGETHER AND FORM A PERFECT SQUARE

A BEAUTIFUL ASSEMBLAGE WHEN SOLVED
THE USUAL TIME LIMIT IS 30 MINUTES

ENTERTAIN YOUR FRIENDS
AN IDEAL GIFT READY FOR MAILING

Copyright 1943 by B. L. Fry, St. Louis, Mo., U. S. A.

This puzzle was also a popular poster.

This machine gun sold
for 29 cents during the
war.

Merrill Publishing's "American Defense Battles Punch-Out Book" was published in 1940 and designed by George Trimmer. Its colorful, one-dimensional, stand up Army, Navy and Air Force action scenes feature late-1930s soldiers and equipment. A number of the cheap dime store soldiers may have been copied from this book.

A rare Marx AA gun.

This paratrooper gun was made of cardboard. A clip was pulled back and a machine gun noise was emitted. This toy was made in Evansville, Indiana.

Toys were out of rubber and tin but soon these materials became critical and wood and cardboard material took over.

Cardboard cutouts were made of the fighting men of all branches.

Children's Comics and Books

Grosset & Dunlap's Air Combat
series was published in nine
volumes by Al Avery.

A guide book was published by
Whitman in 1942 and 1943.

CONSTRUCTION KIT FOR SOLID MODEL

Cadet
BOEING SUPERFORTRESS B-29
¼ SCALE

THE GREAT NEW MECHANICAL NOVELTY & GAME
'ACK-ACK'

SPORT THRILLS FUN

SHOOT AT PLANES IN FLIGHT
It's self-propelled

DOWN A NAZI DIVE-BOMBER

NO CUTTING - NO PASTING   READY TO PUT TOGETHER

ANTI-AIRCRAFT IN ACTION

TORPEDO ACTION GAME

ARMY RAIDERS
VICTORY UNIT
EXTRA HEAVY STOCK

Complete 28 PIECE ACTION SET

23 COMBAT SOLDIERS · JEEP · TANK · TROOP CARRIER · ANTI-AIRCRAFT GUN · MOTORCYCLE RAIDER

THE A. C. GILBERT COMPANY
NEW HAVEN, CONN., U.S.A.
PRINTED IN U.S.A.

ATOMIC BOMB

TOKYO
HIROSHIMA
NAGASAKI

This little game was produced by the well known toy company, The A.C. Gilbert Co. One tried to roll a bee bee in the target. This game was obviously produced after the two atomic bombs were dropped on Japan in August 1945.

AMERICAN RED CROSS WAR FUND CAMPAIGN

KNOX COUNTY 1944

Division_____

Team _____

Report Made By_____

NOTICE---City and Township Chairmen will make all Reports to Campaign Headquarters at the Chamber of Commerce Rooms at the Vincennes City Hall.

Ewing, Printer—Vincennes, Ind.

Even school book covers promoted the war effort. This was put out by the Coca Cola Company.

INDIANA OFFICIAL WAR BALLOT

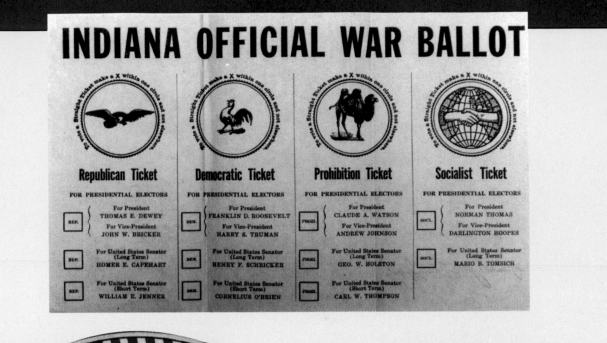

Republican Ticket	Democratic Ticket	Prohibition Ticket	Socialist Ticket
FOR PRESIDENTIAL ELECTORS	FOR PRESIDENTIAL ELECTORS	FOR PRESIDENTIAL ELECTORS	FOR PRESIDENTIAL ELECTORS
For President THOMAS E. DEWEY	For President FRANKLIN D. ROOSEVELT	For President CLAUDE A. WATSON	For President NORMAN THOMAS
For Vice-President JOHN W. BRICKER	For Vice-President HARRY S. TRUMAN	For Vice-President ANDREW JOHNSON	For Vice-President DARLINGTON HOOPES
For United States Senator (Long Term) HOMER E. CAPEHART	For United States Senator (Long Term) HENRY F. SCHRICKER	For United States Senator (Long Term) GEO. W. HOLSTON	For United States Senator (Long Term) MARIO B. TOMSICH
For United States Senator (Short Term) WILLIAM E. JENNER	For United States Senator (Short Term) CORNELIUS O'BRIEN	For United States Senator (Short Term) CARL W. THOMPSON	

WW II SQUADRON PINS

Pets were not forgotten during the wartime effort. They provided companionship for relatives whose sons, husbands, fathers and brothers were away at the front.

Cereal companies joined the war effort. The squadron pins were found inside boxes. The back of many different cereals were used to portray ships, planes, battles and fighting troops.

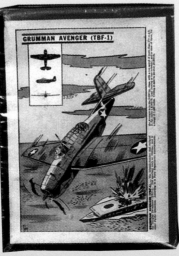

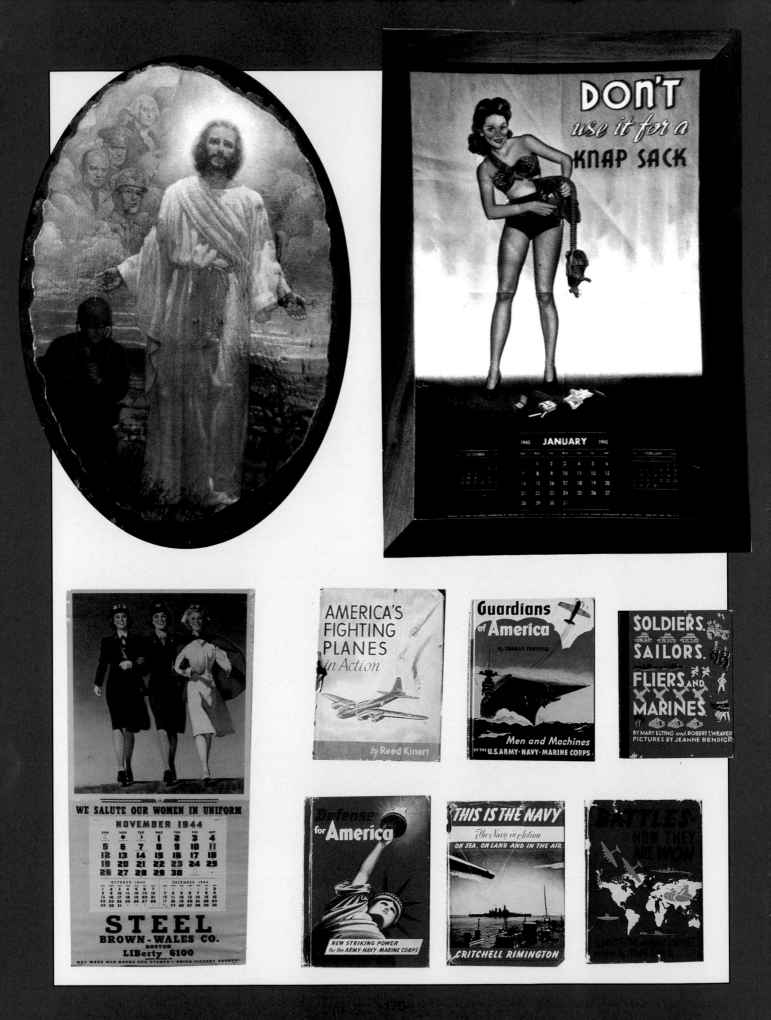

EXHIBIT C

NEW YORK HERALD TRIBUNE EDITORIAL
December 28, 1941

BOY SCOUT DEFENSE PROGRAM

As might be expected, the Boy Scouts of America plan to participate directly in the work of civilian defense. The Scouts in Hawaii have already given a good account of themselves in first aid, messenger service and general usefulness following the bombing of Oahu. New York City Scouts are organized to distribute official air-raid posters. Dr. James E. West, chief Scout executive, announces an Air Scout program whereby boys of fifteen and over may begin training as Air Scout observers, technicians and craftsmen, supplementing such usual Scout activities as signaling, first aid and safety work. Such programs are already in operation in England and Canada. The boys will study airplane engines and instruments, plane identification, navigation, elements of aerodynamics and Civil Aeronautics Administration requirements.

American Scouts will find much of inspiration in the work of the British Boy Scouts, which is graphically described in a pamphlet from London entitled, appropriately, "They Were Prepared." The work of the British boys during bombing raids, fires and blackouts proved invaluable. Growing out of England's experience in two and a quarter years of war, one hundred and eighty different kinds of service jobs are there available to a Scout. More than sixty thousand lads have received National Service medals, many have received Certificates of Gallantry, some have been decorated by the King. Among such jobs are many that are dull and routine; the opportunities for spectacular service will come, we hope, seldom, but the training must go on. As the President put it in his annual Christmas message, "Now, as always, the nation needs citizens who are pledged to keep themselves physically fit, mentally alert and morally straight." We believe that the boys—one and a half million of them in the United States—may be depended on, as may the adults who will be asked, in a campaign beginning next month, to give them the necessary financial support.

V-J DAY
★ ★ ★ ★ ★

· AUGUST 15, 1945 ·

"Japan has surrendered unconditionally in accordance with the terms of the Potsdam Conference."

Harry S. Truman
President of the United States

MANUS

U.S. NAVAL BASE HOSPITAL

This cookie can has a painting of the *USS Idaho* on its cover and other ships on its sides.

The End At Last

About The Contributors

Gary Skoloff in July 1945

Gary Skoloff

Gary Skoloff was born in Newark, New Jersey in 1933. He graduated from Rutgers University and Rutgers Law School. He is a practicing divorce lawyer in Livingston, New Jersey. He lives with his wife Shary in West Orange, New Jersey and on a farm in northeast Pennsylvania.

He grew up in Newark during the war. His older sister's boyfriend served in the military and sent her letters, enclosing military material for Gary. These items launched Gary's obsession with collecting World War II memorabilia.

Like all his peers he collected paper, scrap and savings stamps and was a plane spotter. His collection of homefront items, which makes up a good portion of this book, now numbers over 5,000 items.

He also holds the distinction of being the highest ranking cadet officer in Air Force ROTC in the country not to be commissioned due to overstaffing at the time. He did serve in the US Army, obtaining the rank of corporal.

Martin Jacobs in May 1945

Martin Jacobs

Martin Jacobs was born in San Francisco, California in 1942. He is considered a "War Baby", though he says, he did not get a victory celebration at the time of his birth.

Martin's father served in the 91st Infantry Division during the war and his first collectible was his dad's dog tags. He collected everything he could related to the war all through his school years.

He attended the City College of San Francisco and the University of San Francisco studying creative writing and commercial art. In 1972 he started a mail-order business, "Sports Locker Room" which he ran for 20 years.

In 1992 he concentrated on collecting home front memorabilia and travels extensively to military and collectable shows, always looking for that special "Victory" item.

As a freelance writer he has had feature stories on the home front published in national magazines and newspapers such as *Stars and Stripes, Army and Navy News, Paper Pile, Remember Magazine, Military Trader, Antique Weekly, Collectible Country Americana, Today's Collector,* and some articles for this book.

Jack Matthews and his father
Memorial Day 1941

Jack Matthews

Jack Matthews was born in 1932 and raised in a small town in New England. His father served in the army during World War I and he credits his life-long interest in military history and America's homefront to his upbringing.

From 1954 to 1957 he served as a naval officer aboard the aircraft carrier, *USS Tarawa,* the right ship for Matthews as Tarawa was a famous World War II Pacific battle. He received his Juris Doctor and Master of Law degrees from Georgetown University and practiced communications law as a senior partner in a major Washington, D.C. law firm for 30 years.

Over the past 25 years he has amassed an award-winning collection of antique military tinplate toys and composition figures which has a world-wide reputation. Retiring in his mid-50s, Jack lives on a South Carolina coastal island with his wife Meriam, his dachshund and three cats.

His collection of over 1,000 military toys, games, books and puzzles made during World War II forms the basis for his new book, *"Toys Go To War,"* a pictorial history of the wartime American toy industry.

Jim Osborne in 1953

Jim R. Osborne

Jim R. Osborne has been a Superior Court Judge in Indiana for the past 20 years. A former history teacher, Jim has been an avid collector of everything military related since he was eight years old when a friend of the family gave him a captured German helmet, flag, belt and canteen (this helmet appears in the photo depicting Jim at the time his collection started). Jim was born in June 1945 between VE and VJ Day and recalls some of his earliest interest in military history as being installed as early as age 5 or 6 when his mother and father owned and operated drive-in theatres in Mattoon, Illinois, and in Bloomington, Indiana. During those very early years Jim saw nearly every World War II and post World War II military movie produced. His interest in military history has never waned since that time Jim recalls his father purchasing a Civil War musket when he was in grade school and can remember for years the musket being much taller than he was. Jim continued to collect military artifacts through his high school years and after graduating in 1963 went on to receive a teaching degree in history from Indiana State University in 1967. He then taught history at his alma mater high school in his hometown of Vincennes, Indiana, for four years and during that time continued to assemble an extremely large and impressive collection of artifacts ranging from medals, uniforms, helmets, flags, swords, daggers, firearms and even cannons.

By the time Jim left his teaching position and returned to law school the collection had grown to proportions equivalent to and greater than many military museums. Jim received his law degree from Indiana University in 1974 graduating in the same class with future Vice-President Dan Quayle. He again returned to his home community where he served as a Deputy Prosecutor of Knox County and in 1976 became one of the youngest judges in the state of Indiana.

Over the past 20 years Jim's collection and his interest continued to expand into military vehicles ranging from Jeeps to Sherman tanks. The vehicle and artillery collection became so extensive Jim was encouraged in 1982 to establish the Indiana Military Museum, Inc., a not-for-profit corporation which would allow many of the artifacts Jim has collected to be displayed and enjoyed by others who appreciate such important historical artifacts. The museum houses numerous restored military vehicles and artillery pieces as well as many significant artifacts such as uniforms, equipment, insignia and needless to say, "Victory and Homefront" items, posters and other related memorabilia depicted in this book.

Jim has appeared with many of the vehicles in Hollywood productions including *"The Blues Brothers," "The Road Raiders"* and *"A League of Their Own"* and he and the museum have been topics of coverage on national television programs including CBS' *"America Tonight"* with Bill Geist and *"Good Morning America"* with Joan Lunden.

Ken Fleck

Ken was born after World War II, but his collecting interests were honed by showing off his father's war souvenirs at school. He has had several military collections in the past and since purchasing his first anti-axis piece in 1987 has concentrated on this unusual aspect of the home front. He has amassed, along with his wife, Mady, perhaps the largest collection of this type in the country. Ken has been an ironworker for many years and now works part-time as an auctioneer. The couple live in a suburb of Harrisburg, Pennsylvania.

Ken Fleck in 1951

Merv Bloch in 1945

Merv Bloch

Merv Bloch is a top creative figure in the field of motion picture marketing. Among his many award-winning achievements are the trailers and television commercials for all of Woody Allen's films. Bloch is also a TV documentary producer specializing in World War II subject matter. He is currently developing a series about children in war. His avocation is collecting antique military toys, games, wartime gum cards and propaganda items. He is a native New Yorker, living in Manhattan with his wife and family.

Stan Cohen in 1942

Stan Cohen

The publisher of this book, Stan Cohen is a native of Charleston, West Virginia and a graduate geologist from West Virginia University. He has lived in Missoula, Montana for the past 34 years and was involved in the ski and sporting goods business for 11 years. He was a founder of a local historical museum and recently the Museum of Mountain Flying in Missoula.

He was born in 1938 so has some memories of World War II growing up in the heavily industrial area of Charleston. "My main memories of course," he says, "were the latter years of the war when I played in the blackouts, collected paper and celebrated V-J day." He has been an avid collector of paper ephemera since 1948 when his fourth grade teacher prompted each student to start a collection. Since then he has amassed a large collection of post cards, newspapers, books, world's fair and World War II home front items. His larger collection includes three antique Chevrolets and an antique gas station and general store (front facade only) in his book warehouse.

He has authored or co-authored 48 books and published over 170 since establishing Pictorial Histories in 1976.

Bibliography

Selected Bibliography from Pictorial Histories

Cohen, Stan, *V For Victory, America's Home Front During World War II*, 1991.

_____, *Enemy On Island. Issue in Doubt. The Capture of Wake Island, December 1941*, 1983.

_____, *Destination: Tokyo, A Pictorial History of Doolittle's Tokyo Raid, April 18, 1942*, 1983.

_____, *East Wind Rain, A Pictorial History of the Pearl Harbor Attack*, 1981.

Glynn, Gary, *Montana's Home Front During World War II*, 1994.

Matthews, Jack, *Toys Go To War, World War II Military Toys, Games, Puzzles and Books*, 1995.

McClendon, Dennis E. & Wallace F. Richards, *The Legend of Colin Kelly, America's First Hero of World War II*, 1994.

Young, Don, *December 1941, America's First 25 Days At War*, 1992.